Scripture Alone Rosary

A PRAYER IN COMMON FOR ALL CHRISTIANS

ANDREW SCHMIEDICKE

CHESTERTON PRESS
Strasburg, Virginia

ACKNOWLEDGEMENTS

I pray that this book is an inspiration of the Holy Spirit. Praise be to God for all the good in it. Any mistakes in it are mine.

I thank Bill Vencil for his suggestions on how to conduct theological exchanges with more effective humility and charity. I am grateful to him for meeting with me at the outset of this project to discuss possible Bible translations to use. Bill also gave me valuable feedback toward the completion of this project regarding how to word some parts in the introduction.

I am grateful for my wife's recommendation of the King James Version Bible translation and Bible Illustrations by Gustave Doré which I found at Creationism.org.

I also appreciate my mother-in-law's suggestion about updating some of the archaic words from the KJV Bible.

Finally, I thank my sister-in-law, Anna, for her patient, professional help with the layout and design of this booklet, and the many changes I asked her to make.

Glory to God in the highest! (Luke 2:14)

Contents

Introduction

After a lengthy correspondence discussing and debating the doctrine of *sola scriptura* (scripture alone), I was sitting in church one day musing about it. Gently, quietly, peacefully the question occurred to me, *What would a scripture alone rosary look like?* Considering it to be a prompting of the Holy Spirit, I soon set to work.

The thought occurs to me now that perhaps we Christians sometimes spend too much time discussing and debating the Word of God before adequately praying and pondering the Word of God. One aim of this booklet is to provide an opportunity to do that modeled upon a format developed over the course of the Christian centuries.

A CENTURIES-OLD PRAYER

Catholic Christianity has a centuries-old prayer called the rosary in which one meditates on some of the most significant events in the life, death, and resurrection of Jesus while asking for the prayers of His mother, the Blessed Virgin Mary. Most of these events and prayers are explicitly recorded in scripture while some are only alluded to or deduced from scripture. It is these latter that some Christians find uncomfortable. This prayer booklet is an attempt to remove that obstacle.

Among the various forms it has taken over the centuries, there is a form of the rosary, called the Scriptural Rosary, where a verse or two of scripture is read, and then a request is made to Jesus' mother to pray for us. This booklet follows a similar format, but instead of asking for the prayers of the Blessed Virgin Mary in between the scripture verses, there is a prayer taken directly from the scriptures or based directly on a scripture passage and just reworded into a prayer. Then there is the option of saying the first half of the "Hail Mary" which is taken directly from scripture. It is a combination of the Angel Gabriel's greeting to the Blessed Virgin Mary (called the Angelic Salutation in Luke 1:28), and Elizabeth's response to Mary's greeting at the Visitation in which we see the Holy Spirit fill Elizabeth (Luke 1:41) and inspire her to bless Mary first and then bless the fruit of Mary's womb, Jesus. (Luke 1:42)

In addition, the two events in the Catholic rosary that are not as explicitly recorded in scripture (the Assumption of Mary and the Coronation of Mary), have been replaced by "The Woman Clothed with the Sun" from Revelation 12, and "The Heavenly Jerusalem" from Revelation 21.

By thus consisting solely of events recorded in scripture, scripture verses, and prayers like the "Our Father" and others taken directly from scripture or based directly on scripture, this booklet constitutes a "Scripture Alone" Rosary that should be able to be used by all Christians as a prayer in common.

PRAYER IN COMMON FOR UNITY AMONG CHRISTIANS

It is my hope that this prayer in common will contribute to bringing about the unity of all those who believe in Jesus. As Christians we should be "Endeavouring to keep the unity of the Spirit in the bond of peace." (Ephesians 4:3) For Jesus did not want His disciples divided up into differing doctrines and denominations. Rather, He prayed that all those who believe in Him would be *one* so that the world would believe that He was sent by the Father. *Three times* Jesus prayed for this unity among His disciples on the night before He died for our redemption. (John 17:20-23)

Jesus is our "One Lord." He gave only "one faith"..."one faith, one baptism" (Ephesians 4:5) from "One God and Father of all." (Ephesians 4:6) Jesus died to "gather together in one the children of God that were scattered abroad." (John 11:52) So "there shall be one fold, and one shepherd." (John 10:16) It is my hope that through the use of this booklet as an aid to meditate on the life, death, and glorious resurrection of our One Lord Jesus Christ, we Christians will serve Him by seeking to satisfy His passionate desire for unity among His followers so that the world will believe that the Father sent Him. (John 17:21)

DEEPER DIALOGUE WITH THE DIVINE

Another aim of this booklet is to foster a prayerful dialogue with Jesus. Knowing scripture can help us come to know Jesus Christ. Ignorance of scripture is ignorance of Christ, as St. Jerome once noted, but is knowing scripture enough? (John 5:39) The devil knows scripture. (Matthew 4:6). And he can twist it to deceive us to our own destruction. (2 Peter 3:16) Also, as important as it is for us to know Jesus, scripture passages such as Matthew 7:23, Matthew 25:11-12, and Luke 23:42-43 indicate that it is at least of equal importance that Jesus knows us. One way for us to know Jesus and for Jesus to know us is to enter into dialogue with Him like the woman at the well. (John 4:6-29)

I have tried to arrange the scripture passages and prayers in such a way as to facilitate a dialogue between God and man. For as St. Ambrose notes, we speak to God when we pray; we listen to Him when we read His written Word. The repetitions can be likened to the example of Jesus' prayerful dialogue with His heavenly Father during His agony in the garden when He "prayed the third time, saying the same words." (Matthew 26:44); or how the four mystical creatures in Revelation 4:8 continually say, "Holy, holy, holy, Lord God Almighty" day and night without rest. This is meant to provide an opportunity to persistently set our minds on things above (Colossians 3:2) by regularly calling to mind key events in the life of Jesus and His work of salvation and entering into a prayerful dialogue with Jesus.

PONDERING THE WORD OF GOD AND HIS WORK OF SALVATION

By thus reading, reflecting, and remembering by heart the significant events in the life, death, and resurrection of Jesus Christ as outlined in the rosary and His work of salvation as recorded in the written Word of God, we can, with Mary and like Mary, ponder these events in our hearts (Luke 2:19) and treasure them in our hearts (Luke 2:51) so that Jesus, the Word Incarnate, Who is meek and humble of heart (Matthew 11:29), will transform us by the renewal of our minds and hearts (Ephesians 4:23), making our hearts like His own heart. I can attest from personal experience that praying the rosary and pondering these salvific events led to the renewal of my mind and heart in Christ Jesus.

HOW PRAYING THE ROSARY LED ME BACK TO JESUS

Although my parents in many ways had given me a good Christian upbringing, after a couple of years or so at college I had strayed far from the faith. Generally speaking, I did not pray much, nor read scripture, nor go to church much. Rather, I drifted more and more into living a "fun-loving," pleasure-seeking lifestyle. At one point I was even involved in a kind of spiritualism that affirmed, or at least did not challenge, my loose living. Fortunately, I soon sensed the fleeting, shallow fakeness of it all. But I was spiritually adrift in a secular sea and I did not know where to go. Sometimes I even felt like I was fading from existence.

Then one evening toward the end of my undergraduate years, I drove home to visit my family. I opened the door and walked in on my dad, mom, and various younger brothers and sisters praying the rosary together in the living room. This was new. I didn't remember my family ever doing this when I was growing up.

Feeling like I was intruding on something sacred and intimate, I quietly sat down on the stairs near the living room. I listened to the back-and-forth of the prayers and responses. As I listened, I was struck by the beauty of the prayers and meditations on various events in Jesus' life.

I was so moved that back at college I began praying the rosary practically every day. I delighted in the prayerful dialogue and the meditations on the key events in Jesus' life and His work of salvation. Over the course of the next several months I gradually moved away from a worldly life style and toward a more Christian one. I began reading the scriptures fairly often. I started going to church again and repenting of my sins. I also became involved in Christian works of mercy. As I continued to pray the rosary everyday I increasingly returned to the practice of the faith and committed my life to Jesus as my Lord and Savior in a new way.

In a new way I came to realize that this earthly life is passing away, but Jesus' words will never pass away. (Matthew 24:35) They are the solid rock upon which I can build and live my life. (Matthew 5:24-25) Meditating on His Word, and pondering it in our hearts, like His mother Mary did, will cause it to take root in our hearts and bear fruit a hundred-fold into *eternal* life. Looking back on it, it strikes me that I was something of a lost sheep that the Good Shepherd sought, found, and brought back to His fold by means of the rosary.

An Invitation
So, like Mary and with Mary, let us hear the Word of God and ponder it in our hearts. (Luke 2:19; 11:28) Consider this an invitation to more extensive, deeper dialogue with God and reflection on His Word. Let us meditate on it with Mary, the Mother of Jesus. Let us heed the words of the angel of the Lord in Matthew 1:20. Let us not be afraid to take Mary into our home. Rather, like Joseph and the disciple, John, let us take Mary into our home (Matthew 1:24 & John 19:27) and with her, keep all these things, pondering them in our hearts. I repeat: Let us not be afraid. (Luke 1:30) Rather, let us repent and believe in the Gospel (Mark 1:15), like Mary, the first person recorded in the gospels to hear the Good News and believe it. (Luke 1:30-38, 45) "Blessed are they that hear the word of God, and keep it." (Luke 11:28)

"Lord, teach us to pray!" (Luke 11:1)

Prayer Format
The complete rosary consists of four sets of events, what Catholics call "mysteries": Joyful, Luminous, Sorrowful, and

Glorious. By "mysteries", we mean that through these events God has revealed truth that can be known by pondering them and letting them grow in us like the Word that falls upon good soil in the parable of the sower. (Matthew 13:3-23) Each set consists of five "mysteries" or events each. In this booklet, at the beginning of each set of mysteries/events is an opening prayer based on Acts 2:17-18 asking God to pour out His Spirit.

At the beginning of each event/mystery is its name, and the scripture references to which it corresponds, summarizing it. Then there is the prayer intention for that decade and a scripture verse or two for it. Then the "Our Father" is prayed. Then a short scripture passage pertaining to the event/mystery is read. Then a scriptural prayer taken from a scripture passage is prayed. Then there is the option of saying the first half of the "Hail Mary" which is taken directly from scripture. This format of "read, pray, and say" is done ten times for each event/mystery, thus forming a decade (meaning "ten") of scripture passages and scripture prayers. There are five decades in each of the four sets of events/mysteries.

Then there are two closing prayers to end each decade. First, there is the "Glory to God in the highest" prayer that the angels sing after they announce the birth of Jesus to the shepherds. (Luke 2:14) Then there is a prayer based on Matthew 11:29 asking Jesus to make our hearts like His own meek and humble heart.

At the end of each set of events/mysteries is a closing prayer based on scripture passages from the book of Revelation thanking and praising God.

An alternate format that is closer in style to the Catholic scriptural rosary, but is still scripture alone, is this: Instead of the prayer in between the scripture verses, one just says the first half of the "Hail Mary" which is a combination of the Angelic Salutation and what Elizabeth first says to Mary at their greeting. Alternatively, one could just read the scripture passage and pray the scriptural prayer.

Praying alone. When praying alone, I see one having an opportunity to read and reflect on the scripture passages interspersed with biblical prayers of petition and praise to God.

Praying with a prayer partner. When praying with a prayer partner, one could announce the name of the event/mystery and read the prayer intention and scripture passage for it, then pray the Lord's Prayer. Then the two could alternate: One could read the scripture passage, and then the other could pray the scriptural prayer. And then both could pray the Angelic Salutation and the concluding prayers for each decade together.

Praying in a group. This could work similar to the prayer partner format, except that while one person led the opening prayers of the decade, the rest of the group would pray the scriptural prayer. Then all could say the Angelic Salutation. At the end of each decade the entire group would pray the concluding prayers.

Each set of mysteries takes about 20 minutes to pray. Depending on your schedule, one set of mysteries could be prayed each day or even just one decade per day. Perhaps more could be prayed on the weekends. On Friday it would be appropriate to pray the Sorrowful Mysteries; and on Sunday it would be appropriate to pray the Glorious Mysteries.

The above options are simply suggestions. There are other legitimate ways that the prayer format and schedule could be conducted. For example, even though it is not stated in the prayer format, one could take a moment for extemporaneous prayer after reading the prayer intention and then pray the Lord's Prayer. What's important is to pray from the heart so that you don't just honor God with your lips while your heart is far from Him (Isaiah 29:13).

MINIMIZING DISTRACTIONS

Of course, distractions during prayer are quite common. To help minimize the distractions though, try to picture yourself in the scene with the people who were witnessing the event for the first time. What did they see? What did they hear? What did they think or feel about what they saw and heard? Or try thinking about what you are saying and to whom you are saying it. Say it and pray it—from the heart. If you realize your mind has been wandering, just entrust your thoughts to the meek and humble heart of Jesus and then gently return to reading the scripture passages and slowly saying and praying the prayers. May the Holy Spirit guide you.

For an example of the Holy Spirit guiding and inspiring someone in prayer and praise, let us look at Elizabeth. The holy scriptures tell us that at the sound of Mary's greeting, Elizabeth was *filled with the Holy Spirit* and cried out in a loud voice, "Blessed art thou among women, and blessed is the fruit of thy womb." (Luke 1:41-42) So the Holy Spirit inspires Elizabeth to bless Mary first and then bless Jesus. Why does the Holy Spirit do this? Could it be because in blessing Mary first, Elizabeth will more perfectly bless Jesus by blessing Him in the context of Mary's womb? In any case, we would do well to imitate the example the Holy Spirit has given us in Elizabeth regarding the matter and manner of blessing Jesus.

A note on the biblical translations used in this booklet

For the scripture passages used in this booklet I have used the King James Version (KJV). I decided on this translation for a couple of reasons. First, I wanted to use a translation that was widely respected by non-Catholic Christians. Secondly, in order to avoid having to obtain permission from a publisher of a particular translation of the Bible, I decided to use a translation that was in the public domain. Therefore, to meet both of those criteria I decided on the King James Version. The one exception to this is the scripture passage of the Angelic Salutation. For that I used the 1899 Douay-Rheims American Edition (DRA) translation of the Angel Gabriel's greeting to the Virgin Mary of "Hail, full of grace" which is used in the traditional rendering of the "Hail Mary." Other than that, all the other scripture passages and references are taken from the King James Version of the Bible.[*]

---

[*] In some passages I have changed an archaic usage or spelling to a contemporary one for easier reading. For example: "wast" to "was", "sepulchre" to " sepulcher", "shew" to "show".

Joyful Mysteries

OPENING PRAYER

Oh God, pour out Your Spirit upon all flesh:
on our sons and on our daughters,
and on our young men, and on our old men.

And on Your servants and on Your handmaidens
pour out Your Spirit.
Amen.

(Based on Acts 2:17-18*)*

The Annunciation & the Incarnation

JOHN 1:1, 14; LUKE 1:26-38

Prayer Intention: Humility.
"And whosoever shall exalt himself shall be humbled: and he that shall humble himself shall be exalted." (Matthew 23:12)

...for God resisteth the proud, and giveth grace to the humble. (1 Peter 5:5)

Our Father... (Matthew 6:9-13)

1. **Read:** In the beginning was the Word, and the Word was with God, and the Word was God. (John 1:1)
   Pray: Lord, be it done to me according to Thy word. (Luke 1:38)
   Say: Hail Mary, full of grace, the Lord is with thee. Blessed art thou among women, and blessed is the fruit of thy womb, Jesus. (Luke 1:28 & 42)

2. **Read:** And in the sixth month the angel Gabriel was sent from God unto a city of Galilee, named Nazareth, to a virgin espoused to a man whose name was Joseph, of the house of David; and the virgin's name was Mary. (Luke 1:26-27)
   Pray: Lord, be it done to me according to Thy word. (Luke 1:38)
   Say: Hail Mary, full of grace, the Lord is with thee. Blessed art thou among women, and blessed is the fruit of thy womb, Jesus. (Luke 1:28 & 42)

3. **Read:** And the angel being come in, said unto her: "Hail, full of grace, the Lord is with thee." And when she saw him, she was troubled at his saying, and cast in her mind what manner of salutation this should be. (Luke 1:28-29)
   Pray: Lord, be it done to me according to Thy word. (Luke 1:38)

Say: Hail Mary, full of grace, the Lord is with thee. Blessed art thou among women, and blessed is the fruit of thy womb, Jesus. (Luke 1:28 & 42)

4. **Read:** And the angel said unto her, "Fear not, Mary: for thou hast found favour with God. And, behold, thou shalt conceive in thy womb, and bring forth a Son, and shalt call His name Jesus." (Luke 1:30-31)
   Pray: Lord, be it done to me according to Thy word. (Luke 1:38)
   Say: Hail Mary, full of grace, the Lord is with thee. Blessed art thou among women, and blessed is the fruit of thy womb, Jesus. (Luke 1:28 & 42)

5. **Read:** "He shall be great, and shall be called the Son of the Highest: and the Lord God shall give unto Him the throne of His father David: And He shall reign over the house of Jacob for ever; and of His kingdom there shall be no end." (Luke 1:32-33)
   Pray: Lord, be it done to me according to Thy word. (Luke 1:38)
   Say: Hail Mary, full of grace, the Lord is with thee. Blessed art thou among women, and blessed is the fruit of thy womb, Jesus. (Luke 1:28 & 42)

6. **Read:** Then said Mary unto the angel, "How shall this be, seeing I know not a man?" (Luke 1:34)
   Pray: Lord, be it done to me according to Thy word. (Luke 1:38)
   Say: Hail Mary, full of grace, the Lord is with thee. Blessed art thou among women, and blessed is the fruit of thy womb, Jesus. (Luke 1:28 & 42)

7. **Read:** And the angel answering, said to her: "The Holy Ghost shall come upon thee, and the power of the Most High shall overshadow thee. And therefore also the Holy which shall be born of thee shall be called the Son of God." (Luke 1:35)
   Pray: Lord, be it done to me according to Thy word. (Luke 1:38)

Say: Hail Mary, full of grace, the Lord is with thee. Blessed art thou among women, and blessed is the fruit of thy womb, Jesus. (Luke 1:28 & 42)

8. **Read:** "And, behold, thy cousin Elizabeth, she hath also conceived a son in her old age: and this is the sixth month with her, who was called barren. For with God nothing shall be impossible." (Luke 1:36-37)
   Pray: Lord, be it done to me according to Thy word. (Luke 1:38)
   Say: Hail Mary, full of grace, the Lord is with thee. Blessed art thou among women, and blessed is the fruit of thy womb, Jesus. (Luke 1:28 & 42)

9. **Read:** And Mary said, "Behold the handmaid of the Lord; be it unto me according to thy word." (Luke 1:38)
   Pray: Lord, be it done to me according to Thy word. (Luke 1:38)
   Say: Hail Mary, full of grace, the Lord is with thee. Blessed art thou among women, and blessed is the fruit of thy womb, Jesus. (Luke 1:28 & 42)

10. **Read:** And the Word was made flesh, and dwelt among us. (John 1:14)
    Pray: Lord, be it done to me according to Thy word. (Luke 1:38)
    Say: Hail Mary, full of grace, the Lord is with thee. Blessed art thou among women, and blessed is the fruit of thy womb, Jesus. (Luke 1:28 & 42)

Pray: Glory to God in the highest! (Luke 2:14)

Pray: Oh Jesus, meek and humble of heart, make our hearts like unto Thine. (Based on Matthew 11:29)

The Visitation of Mary & Jesus to Elizabeth & John the Baptist

LUKE 1:39-50, 56

Prayer Intention: Love of neighbor.

"And the second is like unto it, thou shalt love thy neighbor as thyself." (Matthew 22:39)

"A new commandment I give unto you, That ye love one another; as I have loved you, that ye also love one another. By this shall all men know that ye are My disciples, if ye have love one to another." (John 13:34-35)

Our Father... (Matthew 6:9-13)

1. **Read:** And Mary arose in those days, and went into the hill country with haste, into a city of Judah; And entered into the house of Zacharias, and saluted Elizabeth. (Luke 1:39-40)
   Pray: Blessed be the Lord God of Israel; for He has visited and redeemed His people. (Luke 1:68)
   Say: Hail Mary, full of grace, the Lord is with thee. Blessed art thou among women, and blessed is the fruit of thy womb, Jesus. (Luke 1:28 & 42)

2. **Read:** And it came to pass, that when Elizabeth heard the salutation of Mary, the infant leaped in her womb. And Elizabeth was filled with the Holy Ghost: And she cried out with a loud voice, and said: "Blessed art thou among women, and blessed is the fruit of thy womb." (Luke 1:41-42)
   Pray: Blessed be the Lord God of Israel; for He has visited and redeemed His people. (Luke 1:68)
   Say: Hail Mary, full of grace, the Lord is with thee. Blessed art thou among women, and blessed is the fruit of thy womb, Jesus. (Luke 1:28 & 42)

3. **Read:** "And whence is this to me, that the mother of my Lord should come to me?" (Luke 1:43)
   Pray: Blessed be the Lord God of Israel; for He has visited and redeemed His people. (Luke 1:68)
   Say: Hail Mary, full of grace, the Lord is with thee. Blessed art thou among women, and blessed is the fruit of thy womb, Jesus. (Luke 1:28 & 42)

4. **Read:** "For behold as soon as the voice of thy salutation sounded in my ears, the infant in my womb leaped for joy." (Luke 1:44)
   Pray: Blessed be the Lord God of Israel; for He has visited and redeemed His people. (Luke 1:68)
   Say: Hail Mary, full of grace, the Lord is with thee. Blessed art thou among women, and blessed is the fruit of thy womb, Jesus. (Luke 1:28 & 42)

5. **Read:** "And blessed is she that believed: for there shall be a performance of those things which were told her from the Lord." (Luke 1:45)
   Pray: Blessed be the Lord God of Israel; for He has visited and redeemed His people. (Luke 1:68)
   Say: Hail Mary, full of grace, the Lord is with thee. Blessed art thou among women, and blessed is the fruit of thy womb, Jesus. (Luke 1:28 & 42)

6. **Read:** And Mary said, "My soul doth magnify the Lord, And my spirit hath rejoiced in God my Savior." (Luke 1:46-47)
   Pray: Blessed be the Lord God of Israel; for He has visited and redeemed His people. (Luke 1:68)
   Say: Hail Mary, full of grace, the Lord is with thee. Blessed art thou among women, and blessed is the fruit of thy womb, Jesus. (Luke 1:28 & 42)

7. **Read:** "For He hath regarded the low estate of His handmaiden: for, behold, from henceforth all generations shall call me blessed." (Luke 1:48)

Pray: Blessed be the Lord God of Israel; for He has visited and redeemed His people. (Luke 1:68)
Say: Hail Mary, full of grace, the Lord is with thee. Blessed art thou among women, and blessed is the fruit of thy womb, Jesus. (Luke 1:28 & 42)

8. **Read:** "For He that is mighty hath done to me great things; and holy is His name." (Luke 1:49)
Pray: Blessed be the Lord God of Israel; for He has visited and redeemed His people. (Luke 1:68)
Say: Hail Mary, full of grace, the Lord is with thee. Blessed art thou among women, and blessed is the fruit of thy womb, Jesus. (Luke 1:28 & 42)

9. **Read:** "And His mercy is on them that fear Him from generation to generation." (Luke 1:50)
Pray: Blessed be the Lord God of Israel; for He has visited and redeemed His people. (Luke 1:68)
Say: Hail Mary, full of grace, the Lord is with thee. Blessed art thou among women, and blessed is the fruit of thy womb, Jesus. (Luke 1:28 & 42)

10. **Read:** And Mary abode with her about three months, and returned to her own house. (Luke 1:56)
Pray: Blessed be the Lord God of Israel; for He has visited and redeemed His people. (Luke 1:68)
Say: Hail Mary, full of grace, the Lord is with thee. Blessed art thou among women, and blessed is the fruit of thy womb, Jesus. (Luke 1:28 & 42)

Pray: Glory to God in the highest! (Luke 2:14)

Pray: Oh Jesus, meek and humble of heart, make our hearts like unto Thine. (Based on Matthew 11:29)

The Nativity, The Birth of Our Lord Jesus in Bethlehem in a Stable

Luke 2:1, 4-12, 16, 19-20

Prayer Intention: Spirit of poverty.
"Blessed are the poor in spirit: for theirs is the kingdom of heaven."
(Matthew 5:3)

Our Father... (Matthew 6:9-13)

1. **Read:** And it came to pass in those days, that there went out a decree from Caesar Augustus that all the world should be taxed. (Luke 2:1)
    Pray: Glory to God in the highest, and on earth peace, good will toward men! (Luke 2:14)
    Say: Hail Mary, full of grace, the Lord is with thee. Blessed art thou among women, and blessed is the fruit of thy womb, Jesus. (Luke 1:28 & 42)

2. **Read:** And Joseph also went up from Galilee, out of the city of Nazareth, into Judaea, unto the city of David, which is called Bethlehem; (because he was of the house and lineage of David:) To be taxed with Mary his espoused wife, being great with Child. (Luke 2:4-5)
    Pray: Glory to God in the highest, and on earth peace, good will toward men! (Luke 2:14)
    Say: Hail Mary, full of grace, the Lord is with thee. Blessed art thou among women, and blessed is the fruit of thy womb, Jesus. (Luke 1:28 & 42)

3. **Read:** And so it was, that, while they were there, the days were accomplished that she should be delivered. And she brought forth her firstborn Son, and wrapped Him in

swaddling clothes, and laid Him in a manger; because there was no room for them in the inn. (Luke 2:6-7)
Pray: Glory to God in the highest, and on earth peace, good will toward men! (Luke 2:14)
Say: Hail Mary, full of grace, the Lord is with thee. Blessed art thou among women, and blessed is the fruit of thy womb, Jesus. (Luke 1:28 & 42)

4. **Read:** And there were in the same country shepherds abiding in the field, keeping watch over their flock by night. (Luke 2:8)
    Pray: Glory to God in the highest, and on earth peace, good will toward men! (Luke 2:14)
    Say: Hail Mary, full of grace, the Lord is with thee. Blessed art thou among women, and blessed is the fruit of thy womb, Jesus. (Luke 1:28 & 42)

5. **Read:** And, lo, the angel of the Lord came upon them, and the glory of the Lord shone round about them: and they were sore afraid. (Luke 2:9)
    Pray: Glory to God in the highest, and on earth peace, good will toward men! (Luke 2:14)
    Say: Hail Mary, full of grace, the Lord is with thee. Blessed art thou among women, and blessed is the fruit of thy womb, Jesus. (Luke 1:28 & 42)

6. **Read:** And the angel said unto them, "Fear not: for, behold, I bring you good tidings of great joy, which shall be to all people." (Luke 2:10)
    Pray: Glory to God in the highest, and on earth peace, good will toward men! (Luke 2:14)
    Say: Hail Mary, full of grace, the Lord is with thee. Blessed art thou among women, and blessed is the fruit of thy womb, Jesus. (Luke 1:28 & 42)

7. **Read:** "For unto you is born this day in the city of David a Saviour, which is Christ the Lord. And this shall be a sign

unto you: Ye shall find the Babe wrapped in swaddling clothes, lying in a manger." (Luke 2:11-12)

Pray: Glory to God in the highest, and on earth peace, good will toward men! (Luke 2:14)

Say: Hail Mary, full of grace, the Lord is with thee. Blessed art thou among women, and blessed is the fruit of thy womb, Jesus. (Luke 1:28 & 42)

8. **Read:** And they came with haste, and found Mary, and Joseph, and the Babe lying in a manger. (Luke 2:16)

    Pray: Glory to God in the highest, and on earth peace, good will toward men! (Luke 2:14)

    Say: Hail Mary, full of grace, the Lord is with thee. Blessed art thou among women, and blessed is the fruit of thy womb, Jesus. (Luke 1:28 & 42)

9. **Read:** But Mary kept all these things, and pondered them in her heart. (Luke 2:19)

    Pray: Glory to God in the highest, and on earth peace, good will toward men! (Luke 2:14)

    Say: Hail Mary, full of grace, the Lord is with thee. Blessed art thou among women, and blessed is the fruit of thy womb, Jesus. (Luke 1:28 & 42)

10. **Read:** And the shepherds returned, glorifying and praising God for all the things that they had heard and seen, as it was told unto them. (Luke 2:20)

    Pray: Glory to God in the highest, and on earth peace, good will toward men! (Luke 2:14)

    Say: Hail Mary, full of grace, the Lord is with thee. Blessed art thou among women, and blessed is the fruit of thy womb, Jesus. (Luke 1:28 & 42)

Pray: Glory to God in the highest! (Luke 2:14)

Pray: Oh Jesus, meek and humble of heart, make our hearts like unto Thine. (Based on Matthew 11:29)

Joseph and Mary present Jesus in the Temple
LUKE 2:22, 25-32, 34-35, 39-40

Prayer Intention: Purity of heart.
"Blessed are the pure in heart: for they shall see God." (Matthew 5:8)

Our Father... (Matthew 6:9-13)

1. **Read:** And when the days of her purification according to the law of Moses were accomplished, they brought [Jesus] to Jerusalem, to present Him to the Lord. (Luke 2:22)
   Pray: Lord, give light to those who sit in darkness and in the shadow of death, and guide our feet into the way of peace. (Luke 1:79)
   Say: Hail Mary, full of grace, the Lord is with thee. Blessed art thou among women, and blessed is the fruit of thy womb, Jesus. (Luke 1:28 & 42)

2. **Read:** And, behold, there was a man in Jerusalem, whose name was Simeon; and the same man was just and devout, waiting for the consolation of Israel: and the Holy Ghost was upon him. (Luke 2:25)
   Pray: Lord, give light to those who sit in darkness and in the shadow of death, and guide our feet into the way of peace. (Luke 1:79)
   Say: Hail Mary, full of grace, the Lord is with thee. Blessed art thou among women, and blessed is the fruit of thy womb, Jesus. (Luke 1:28 & 42)

3. **Read:** And it was revealed unto him by the Holy Ghost, that he should not see death, before he had seen the Lord's Christ. (Luke 2:26)
   Pray: Lord, give light to those who sit in darkness and in the shadow of death, and guide our feet into the way of peace. (Luke 1:79)

Say: Hail Mary, full of grace, the Lord is with thee. Blessed art thou among women, and blessed is the fruit of thy womb, Jesus. (Luke 1:28 & 42)

4. **Read:** And he came by the Spirit into the temple: and when the parents brought in the Child Jesus, to do for Him after the custom of the law, then he took Him up in his arms, and blessed God. (Luke 2:27-28)
   Pray: Lord, give light to those who sit in darkness and in the shadow of death, and guide our feet into the way of peace. (Luke 1:79)
   Say: Hail Mary, full of grace, the Lord is with thee. Blessed art thou among women, and blessed is the fruit of thy womb, Jesus. (Luke 1:28 & 42)

5. **Read:** [He said] "Lord, now let Thou Thy servant depart in peace, according to Thy word:" (Luke 2:29)
   Pray: Lord, give light to those who sit in darkness and in the shadow of death, and guide our feet into the way of peace. (Luke 1:79)
   Say: Hail Mary, full of grace, the Lord is with thee. Blessed art thou among women, and blessed is the fruit of thy womb, Jesus. (Luke 1:28 & 42)

6. **Read:** "For mine eyes have seen Thy salvation, which Thou hast prepared before the face of all people;" (Luke 2:30-31)
   Pray: Lord, give light to those who sit in darkness and in the shadow of death, and guide our feet into the way of peace. (Luke 1:79)
   Say: Hail Mary, full of grace, the Lord is with thee. Blessed art thou among women, and blessed is the fruit of thy womb, Jesus. (Luke 1:28 & 42)

7. **Read:** "A light to lighten the Gentiles, and the glory of Thy people Israel." (Luke 2:32)
   Pray: Lord, give light to those who sit in darkness and in the shadow of death, and guide our feet into the way of peace. (Luke 1:79)

Say: Hail Mary, full of grace, the Lord is with thee. Blessed art thou among women, and blessed is the fruit of thy womb, Jesus. (Luke 1:28 & 42)

8. **Read:** And Simeon blessed them, and said unto Mary His mother, "Behold, this Child is set for the fall and rising again of many in Israel; and for a sign which shall be spoken against; (Yea, a sword shall pierce through thy own soul also,) that the thoughts of many hearts may be revealed." (Luke 2:34-35)
   Pray: Lord, give light to those who sit in darkness and in the shadow of death, and guide our feet into the way of peace. (Luke 1:79)
   Say: Hail Mary, full of grace, the Lord is with thee. Blessed art thou among women, and blessed is the fruit of thy womb, Jesus. (Luke 1:28 & 42)

9. **Read:** And when they had performed all things according to the law of the Lord, they returned into Galilee, to their own city Nazareth. (Luke 2:39)
   Pray: Lord, give light to those who sit in darkness and in the shadow of death, and guide our feet into the way of peace. (Luke 1:79)
   Say: Hail Mary, full of grace, the Lord is with thee. Blessed art thou among women, and blessed is the fruit of thy womb, Jesus. (Luke 1:28 & 42)

10. **Read:** And the Child grew, and waxed strong in spirit, filled with wisdom: and the grace of God was upon Him. (Luke 2:40)
    Pray: Lord, give light to those who sit in darkness and in the shadow of death, and guide our feet into the way of peace. (Luke 1:79)
    Say: Hail Mary, full of grace, the Lord is with thee. Blessed art thou among women, and blessed is the fruit of thy womb, Jesus. (Luke 1:28 & 42)

Pray: Glory to God in the highest! (Luke 2:14)

Pray: Oh Jesus, meek and humble of heart, make our hearts like unto Thine. (Based on Matthew 11:29)

The Finding of Jesus in the Temple
LUKE 2:41-52

Prayer Intention: Wisdom.
If any of you lack wisdom, let him ask of God, that giveth to all men liberally, and upbraideth not; and it shall be given him. (James 1:5)

Our Father... (Matthew 6:9-13)

1. **Read:** Now His parents went to Jerusalem every year at the feast of the Passover. And when He was twelve years old, they went up to Jerusalem after the custom of the feast. (Luke 2:41-42)
   Pray: Lord, give knowledge of salvation to Thy people. (Luke 1:77)
   Say: Hail Mary, full of grace, the Lord is with thee. Blessed art thou among women, and blessed is the fruit of thy womb, Jesus. (Luke 1:28 & 42)

2. **Read:** And when they had fulfilled the days, as they returned, the Child Jesus tarried behind in Jerusalem; and Joseph and His mother knew not of it. (Luke 2:43)
   Pray: Lord, give knowledge of salvation to Thy people. (Luke 1:77)
   Say: Hail Mary, full of grace, the Lord is with thee. Blessed art thou among women, and blessed is the fruit of thy womb, Jesus. (Luke 1:28 & 42)

3. **Read:** But they, supposing Him to have been in the company, went a day's journey; and they sought Him among their kinsfolk and acquaintance. (Luke 2:44)
   Pray: Lord, give knowledge of salvation to Thy people. (Luke 1:77)

Say: Hail Mary, full of grace, the Lord is with thee. Blessed art thou among women, and blessed is the fruit of thy womb, Jesus. (Luke 1:28 & 42)

4. **Read:** And when they found Him not, they turned back again to Jerusalem, seeking Him. (Luke 2:45)
   Pray: Lord, give knowledge of salvation to Thy people. (Luke 1:77)
   Say: Hail Mary, full of grace, the Lord is with thee. Blessed art thou among women, and blessed is the fruit of thy womb, Jesus. (Luke 1:28 & 42)

5. **Read:** And it came to pass, that after three days they found Him in the temple, sitting in the midst of the doctors, both hearing them, and asking them questions. (Luke 2:46)
   Pray: Lord, give knowledge of salvation to Thy people. (Luke 1:77)
   Say: Hail Mary, full of grace, the Lord is with thee. Blessed art thou among women, and blessed is the fruit of thy womb, Jesus. (Luke 1:28 & 42)

6. **Read:** And all that heard Him were astonished at His understanding and answers. (Luke 2:47)
   Pray: Lord, give knowledge of salvation to Thy people. (Luke 1:77)
   Say: Hail Mary, full of grace, the Lord is with thee. Blessed art thou among women, and blessed is the fruit of thy womb, Jesus. (Luke 1:28 & 42)

7. **Read:** And when they saw Him, they were amazed: and His mother said unto Him, "Son, why hast Thou thus dealt with us? Behold, Thy father and I have sought Thee sorrowing." (Luke 2:48)
   Pray: Lord, give knowledge of salvation to Thy people. (Luke 1:77)

Say: Hail Mary, full of grace, the Lord is with thee. Blessed art thou among women, and blessed is the fruit of thy womb, Jesus. (Luke 1:28 & 42)

8. **Read:** And He said to them: "How is it that you sought Me? Did you not know, that I must be about My Father's business?" And they understood not the word that He spoke unto them. (Luke 2:49-50)
   Pray: Lord, give knowledge of salvation to Thy people. (Luke 1:77)
   Say: Hail Mary, full of grace, the Lord is with thee. Blessed art thou among women, and blessed is the fruit of thy womb, Jesus. (Luke 1:28 & 42)

9. **Read:** And He went down with them, and came to Nazareth, and was subject unto them: but His mother kept all these sayings in her heart. (Luke 2:51)
   Pray: Lord, give knowledge of salvation to Thy people. (Luke 1:77)
   Say: Hail Mary, full of grace, the Lord is with thee. Blessed art thou among women, and blessed is the fruit of thy womb, Jesus. (Luke 1:28 & 42)

10. **Read:** And Jesus increased in wisdom and stature, and in favour with God and man. (Luke 2:52)
    Pray: Lord, give knowledge of salvation to Thy people. (Luke 1:77)
    Say: Hail Mary, full of grace, the Lord is with thee. Blessed art thou among women, and blessed is the fruit of thy womb, Jesus. (Luke 1:28 & 42)

Pray: Glory to God in the highest! (Luke 2:14)

Pray: Oh Jesus, meek and humble of heart, make our hearts like unto Thine. (Based on Matthew 11:29)

CLOSING PRAYER

We give Thee thanks, O Lord God Almighty,
Who is, and was, and is to come.
(Revelation 11:17)

Great and marvelous are Thy works,
Lord God Almighty;
just and true are Thy ways, Thou King of saints.
(Revelation 15:3)

Praise our God, all ye His servants,
and ye that fear Him, both small and great.
(Revelation 19:5)

Amen.
Even so, come, Lord Jesus.
The grace of our Lord Jesus Christ be with you all.
Amen.
(Revelation 22:20-21)

Luminous Mysteries

OPENING PRAYER

Oh God, pour out Your Spirit upon all flesh:
on our sons and on our daughters,
and on our young men, and on our old men.

And on Your servants and on Your handmaidens
pour out Your Spirit.
Amen.

(Based on Acts 2:17-18*)*

The Baptism of Jesus

Matthew 3:1-2, 5-6, 11, 13-17

Prayer Intention: Repentance.

Jesus answered, "Verily, verily, I say unto thee, Except a man be born of water and of the Spirit, he cannot enter into the kingdom of God." (John 3:5)

Then Peter said unto them, "Repent, and be baptized every one of you in the name of Jesus Christ for the remission of sins, and ye shall receive the gift of the Holy Ghost." (Acts 2:38)

Our Father... (Matthew 6:9-13)

1. **Read:** In those days came John the Baptist, preaching in the wilderness of Judaea, And saying, "Repent ye: for the kingdom of heaven is at hand!" (Matthew 3:1-2)
   Pray: O God, wash me, and I shall be whiter than snow. (Psalm 51:7)
   Say: Hail Mary, full of grace, the Lord is with thee. Blessed art thou among women, and blessed is the fruit of thy womb, Jesus. (Luke 1:28 & 42)

2. **Read:** Then went out to him Jerusalem, and all Judaea, and all the region round about Jordan, And were baptized of him in Jordan, confessing their sins. (Matthew 3:5-6)
   Pray: O God, wash me, and I shall be whiter than snow. (Psalm 51:7)
   Say: Hail Mary, full of grace, the Lord is with thee. Blessed art thou among women, and blessed is the fruit of thy womb, Jesus. (Luke 1:28 & 42)

3. **Read:** [He said] "I indeed baptize you with water unto repentance, but He that cometh after me is mightier than I." (Matthew 3:11a)
   Pray: O God, wash me, and I shall be whiter than snow. (Psalm 51:7)
   Say: Hail Mary, full of grace, the Lord is with thee. Blessed art thou among women, and blessed is the fruit of thy womb, Jesus. (Luke 1:28 & 42)

4. **Read:** "He shall baptize you with the Holy Ghost, and with fire." (Matthew 3:11c)
   Pray: O God, wash me, and I shall be whiter than snow. (Psalm 51:7)
   Say: Hail Mary, full of grace, the Lord is with thee. Blessed art thou among women, and blessed is the fruit of thy womb, Jesus. (Luke 1:28 & 42)

5. **Read:** Then cometh Jesus from Galilee to the Jordan, unto John, to be baptized by him. (Matthew 3:13)
   Pray: O God, wash me, and I shall be whiter than snow. (Psalm 51:7)
   Say: Hail Mary, full of grace, the Lord is with thee. Blessed art thou among women, and blessed is the fruit of thy womb, Jesus. (Luke 1:28 & 42)

6. **Read:** But John stayed Him, saying: "I ought to be baptized by Thee, and comest Thou to me?" (Matthew 3:14)
   Pray: O God, wash me, and I shall be whiter than snow. (Psalm 51:7)
   Say: Hail Mary, full of grace, the Lord is with thee. Blessed art thou among women, and blessed is the fruit of thy womb, Jesus. (Luke 1:28 & 42)

7. **Read:** And Jesus answering said unto him, "[Allow] it to be so now: for thus it becometh us to fulfill all righteousness." (Matthew 3:15a)

Pray: O God, wash me, and I shall be whiter than snow. (Psalm 51:7)

Say: Hail Mary, full of grace, the Lord is with thee. Blessed art thou among women, and blessed is the fruit of thy womb, Jesus. (Luke 1:28 & 42)

8. **Read:** Then [John allowed] Him. (Matthew 3:15b)

   Pray: O God, wash me, and I shall be whiter than snow. (Psalm 51:7)

   Say: Hail Mary, full of grace, the Lord is with thee. Blessed art thou among women, and blessed is the fruit of thy womb, Jesus. (Luke 1:28 & 42)

9. **Read:** And Jesus, when He was baptized, went up straightway out of the water: and, lo, the heavens were opened unto Him, and [John] saw the Spirit of God descending like a dove, and lighting upon Him. (Matthew 3:16)

   Pray: O God, wash me, and I shall be whiter than snow. (Psalm 51:7)

   Say: Hail Mary, full of grace, the Lord is with thee. Blessed art thou among women, and blessed is the fruit of thy womb, Jesus. (Luke 1:28 & 42)

10. **Read:** And lo a voice from heaven, saying, "This is My beloved Son, in Whom I am well pleased." (Matthew 3:17)

    Pray: O God, wash me, and I shall be whiter than snow. (Psalm 51:7)

    Say: Hail Mary, full of grace, the Lord is with thee. Blessed art thou among women, and blessed is the fruit of thy womb, Jesus. (Luke 1:28 & 42)

Pray: Glory to God in the highest! (Luke 2:14)

Pray: Oh Jesus, meek and humble of heart, make our hearts like unto Thine. (Based on Matthew 11:29)

The Marriage Feast at Cana
THE FIRST PUBLIC MIRACLE OF JESUS
JOHN 2:1-11

Prayer Intention: Holy, life-long marriages.

"But from the beginning of the creation God made them male and female. For this cause shall a man leave his father and mother, and cleave to his wife; And they two shall be one flesh: so then they are no more two, but one flesh. What therefore God hath joined together, let not man put asunder." (Mark 10:6-9)

Our Father... (Matthew 6:9-13)

1. **Read:** And the third day there was a marriage in Cana of Galilee; and the mother of Jesus was there. (John 2:1)
    Pray: Lord, make all things new. (Revelation 21:5)
    Say: Hail Mary, full of grace, the Lord is with thee. Blessed art thou among women, and blessed is the fruit of thy womb, Jesus. (Luke 1:28 & 42)

2. **Read:** And both Jesus was called, and His disciples, to the marriage. (John 2:2)
    Pray: Lord, make all things new. (Revelation 21:5)
    Say: Hail Mary, full of grace, the Lord is with thee. Blessed art thou among women, and blessed is the fruit of thy womb, Jesus. (Luke 1:28 & 42)

3. **Read:** And when they wanted wine, the mother of Jesus said unto Him, "They have no wine." (John 2:3)
    Pray: Lord, make all things new. (Revelation 21:5)
    Say: Hail Mary, full of grace, the Lord is with thee. Blessed art thou among women, and blessed is the fruit of thy womb, Jesus. (Luke 1:28 & 42)

4. **Read:** Jesus said unto her, "Woman, what have I to do with thee? Mine hour is not yet come." (John 2:4)
   Pray: Lord, make all things new. (Revelation 21:5)
   Say: Hail Mary, full of grace, the Lord is with thee. Blessed art thou among women, and blessed is the fruit of thy womb, Jesus. (Luke 1:28 & 42)

5. **Read:** His mother said unto the servants, "Whatsoever He saith unto you, do it." (John 2:5)
   Pray: Lord, make all things new. (Revelation 21:5)
   Say: Hail Mary, full of grace, the Lord is with thee. Blessed art thou among women, and blessed is the fruit of thy womb, Jesus. (Luke 1:28 & 42)

6. **Read:** Now there were set there six waterpots of stone, according to the manner of the purifying of the Jews, containing two or three measures apiece. (John 2:6)
   Pray: Lord, make all things new. (Revelation 21:5)
   Say: Hail Mary, full of grace, the Lord is with thee. Blessed art thou among women, and blessed is the fruit of thy womb, Jesus. (Luke 1:28 & 42)

7. **Read:** Jesus saith to them: "Fill the waterpots with water." And they filled them up to the brim. (John 2:7)
   Pray: Lord, make all things new. (Revelation 21:5)
   Say: Hail Mary, full of grace, the Lord is with thee. Blessed art thou among women, and blessed is the fruit of thy womb, Jesus. (Luke 1:28 & 42)

8. **Read:** And He saith unto them, "Draw out now, and [take it] unto the governor of the feast." And they [took] it. (John 2:8)
   Pray: Lord, make all things new. (Revelation 21:5)
   Say: Hail Mary, full of grace, the Lord is with thee. Blessed art thou among women, and blessed is the fruit of thy womb, Jesus. (Luke 1:28 & 42)

9. **Read:** When the ruler of the feast had tasted the water that was made wine, and knew not whence it was: (but the servants which drew the water knew;) the governor of the feast called the bridegroom, (John 2:9)

   Pray: Lord, make all things new. (Revelation 21:5)

   Say: Hail Mary, full of grace, the Lord is with thee. Blessed art thou among women, and blessed is the fruit of thy womb, Jesus. (Luke 1:28 & 42)

10. **Read:** And saith unto him, "Every man at the beginning doth set forth good wine; and when men have well drunk, then that which is worse: but thou hast kept the good wine until now." This beginning of miracles did Jesus in Cana of Galilee, and manifested forth His glory; and His disciples believed on Him. (John 2:10-11)

    Pray: Lord, make all things new. (Revelation 21:5)

    Say: Hail Mary, full of grace, the Lord is with thee. Blessed art thou among women, and blessed is the fruit of thy womb, Jesus. (Luke 1:28 & 42)

Pray: Glory to God in the highest! (Luke 2:14)

Pray: Oh Jesus, meek and humble of heart, make our hearts like unto Thine. (Based on Matthew 11:29)

The Proclamation of the Gospel and the Spread of the Kingdom of God

MATTHEW 4:17, 23; 10:5A, 7-8, 22; MARK 6:7, 13;
LUKE 9:6; 10:1, 9

Prayer Intention: That the Lord of the harvest send laborers into His harvest.

But when He saw the multitudes, He was moved with compassion on them, because they fainted, and were scattered abroad, as sheep having no shepherd. Then saith He unto His disciples, "The harvest truly is plenteous, but the laborers are few; Pray ye therefore the Lord of the harvest, that He will send forth laborers into His harvest." (Matthew 9:36-38)

Our Father... (Matthew 6:9-13)

1. **Read:** From that time Jesus began to preach, and to say, "Repent: for the kingdom of heaven is at hand." (Matthew 4:17)
   Pray: Lord of the harvest, send forth laborers into Your harvest. (Matthew 9:38)
   Say: Hail Mary, full of grace, the Lord is with thee. Blessed art thou among women, and blessed is the fruit of thy womb, Jesus. (Luke 1:28 & 42)

2. **Read:** And Jesus went about all Galilee, teaching in their synagogues, and preaching the gospel of the kingdom, and healing all manner of sickness and all manner of disease among the people. (Matthew 4:23)
   Pray: Lord of the harvest, send forth laborers into Your harvest. (Matthew 9:38)
   Say: Hail Mary, full of grace, the Lord is with thee. Blessed art thou among women, and blessed is the fruit of thy womb, Jesus. (Luke 1:28 & 42)

3. **Read:** And He called unto Him the Twelve, and began to send them forth by two and two; and gave them power over unclean spirits. (Mark 6:7)
Pray: Lord of the harvest, send forth laborers into Your harvest. (Matthew 9:38)
Say: Hail Mary, full of grace, the Lord is with thee. Blessed art thou among women, and blessed is the fruit of thy womb, Jesus. (Luke 1:28 & 42)

4. **Read:** These twelve Jesus sent forth, and commanded them, saying, "...And as ye go, preach, saying, The kingdom of heaven is at hand." (Matthew 10:5a & 7)
Pray: Lord of the harvest, send forth laborers into Your harvest. (Matthew 9:38)
Say: Hail Mary, full of grace, the Lord is with thee. Blessed art thou among women, and blessed is the fruit of thy womb, Jesus. (Luke 1:28 & 42)

5. **Read:** "Heal the sick, cleanse the lepers, raise the dead, cast out devils: freely ye have received, freely give." (Matthew 10:8)
Pray: Lord of the harvest, send forth laborers into Your harvest. (Matthew 9:38)
Say: Hail Mary, full of grace, the Lord is with thee. Blessed art thou among women, and blessed is the fruit of thy womb, Jesus. (Luke 1:28 & 42)

6. **Read:** And they departed, and went through the towns, preaching the gospel, and healing every where. (Luke 9:6)
Pray: Lord of the harvest, send forth laborers into Your harvest. (Matthew 9:38)
Say: Hail Mary, full of grace, the Lord is with thee. Blessed art thou among women, and blessed is the fruit of thy womb, Jesus. (Luke 1:28 & 42)

7. **Read:** And they cast out many devils, and anointed with oil many that were sick, and healed them. (Mark 6:13)

Pray: Lord of the harvest, send forth laborers into Your harvest. (Matthew 9:38)

Say: Hail Mary, full of grace, the Lord is with thee. Blessed art thou among women, and blessed is the fruit of thy womb, Jesus. (Luke 1:28 & 42)

8. **Read:** After these things the Lord appointed other seventy also, and sent them two and two before His face into every city and place, whither He Himself would come. (Luke 10:1)

   Pray: Lord of the harvest, send forth laborers into Your harvest. (Matthew 9:38)

   Say: Hail Mary, full of grace, the Lord is with thee. Blessed art thou among women, and blessed is the fruit of thy womb, Jesus. (Luke 1:28 & 42)

9. **Read:** "And heal the sick that are therein, and say unto them, 'The kingdom of God is come nigh unto you.'" (Luke 10:9)

   Pray: Lord of the harvest, send forth laborers into Your harvest. (Matthew 9:38)

   Say: Hail Mary, full of grace, the Lord is with thee. Blessed art thou among women, and blessed is the fruit of thy womb, Jesus. (Luke 1:28 & 42)

10. **Read:** "And ye shall be hated of all men for My Name's sake: but he that endureth to the end shall be saved." (Matthew 10:22)

    Pray: Lord of the harvest, send forth laborers into Your harvest. (Matthew 9:38)

    Say: Hail Mary, full of grace, the Lord is with thee. Blessed art thou among women, and blessed is the fruit of thy womb, Jesus. (Luke 1:28 & 42)

Pray: Glory to God in the highest! (Luke 2:14)

Pray: Oh Jesus, meek and humble of heart, make our hearts like unto Thine. (Based on Matthew 11:29)

The Transfiguration of Jesus
MATTHEW 17:1-9

Prayer Intention: Reverence for God.
Wherefore we receiving a kingdom which cannot be moved, let us have grace, whereby we may serve God acceptably with reverence and godly fear. (Hebrews 12:28)

Our Father... (Matthew 6:9-13)

1. **Read:** And after six days Jesus took Peter, James, and John his brother, and brought them up into a high mountain apart. (Matthew 17:1)
   Pray: Holy, holy, holy, Lord God Almighty, which was, and is, and is to come! (Revelation 4:8)
   Say: Hail Mary, full of grace, the Lord is with thee. Blessed art thou among women, and blessed is the fruit of thy womb, Jesus. (Luke 1:28 & 42)

2. **Read:** And [He] was transfigured before them: and His face did shine as the sun, and His raiment was white as the light. (Matthew 17:2)
   Pray: Holy, holy, holy, Lord God Almighty, which was, and is, and is to come! (Revelation 4:8)
   Say: Hail Mary, full of grace, the Lord is with thee. Blessed art thou among women, and blessed is the fruit of thy womb, Jesus. (Luke 1:28 & 42)

3. **Read:** And, behold, there appeared unto them Moses and Elias talking with Him. (Matthew 17:3)
   Pray: Holy, holy, holy, Lord God Almighty, which was, and is, and is to come! (Revelation 4:8)

Say: Hail Mary, full of grace, the Lord is with thee. Blessed art thou among women, and blessed is the fruit of thy womb, Jesus. (Luke 1:28 & 42)

4. **Read:** Then answered Peter, and said unto Jesus, "Lord, it is good for us to be here: if Thou will, let us make here three tabernacles; one for Thee, and one for Moses, and one for Elias." (Matthew 17:4)

   Pray: Holy, holy, holy, Lord God Almighty, which was, and is, and is to come! (Revelation 4:8)

   Say: Hail Mary, full of grace, the Lord is with thee. Blessed art thou among women, and blessed is the fruit of thy womb, Jesus. (Luke 1:28 & 42)

5. **Read:** While he yet spoke, behold, a bright cloud overshadowed them. (Matthew 17:5a)

   Pray: Holy, holy, holy, Lord God Almighty, which was, and is, and is to come! (Revelation 4:8)

   Say: Hail Mary, full of grace, the Lord is with thee. Blessed art thou among women, and blessed is the fruit of thy womb, Jesus. (Luke 1:28 & 42)

6. **Read:** And behold a voice out of the cloud, which said, "This is My beloved Son, in Whom I am well pleased; hear ye Him." (Matthew 17:5b)

   Pray: Holy, holy, holy, Lord God Almighty, which was, and is, and is to come! (Revelation 4:8)

   Say: Hail Mary, full of grace, the Lord is with thee. Blessed art thou among women, and blessed is the fruit of thy womb, Jesus. (Luke 1:28 & 42)

7. **Read:** And when the disciples heard it, they fell on their face, and were sore afraid. (Matthew 17:6)

   Pray: Holy, holy, holy, Lord God Almighty, which was, and is, and is to come! (Revelation 4:8)

Say: Hail Mary, full of grace, the Lord is with thee. Blessed art thou among women, and blessed is the fruit of thy womb, Jesus. (Luke 1:28 & 42)

8. **Read:** And Jesus came and touched them, and said, "Arise, and be not afraid." (Matthew 17:7)
   Pray: Holy, holy, holy, Lord God Almighty, which was, and is, and is to come! (Revelation 4:8)
   Say: Hail Mary, full of grace, the Lord is with thee. Blessed art thou among women, and blessed is the fruit of thy womb, Jesus. (Luke 1:28 & 42)

9. **Read:** And when they had lifted up their eyes, they saw no man, save Jesus only. (Matthew 17:8)
   Pray: Holy, holy, holy, Lord God Almighty, which was, and is, and is to come! (Revelation 4:8)
   Say: Hail Mary, full of grace, the Lord is with thee. Blessed art thou among women, and blessed is the fruit of thy womb, Jesus. (Luke 1:28 & 42)

10. **Read:** And as they came down from the mountain, Jesus charged them, saying, "Tell the vision to no man, until the Son of Man be risen again from the dead." (Matthew 17:9)
    Pray: Holy, holy, holy, Lord God Almighty, which was, and is, and is to come! (Revelation 4:8)
    Say: Hail Mary, full of grace, the Lord is with thee. Blessed art thou among women, and blessed is the fruit of thy womb, Jesus. (Luke 1:28 & 42)

Pray: Glory to God in the highest! (Luke 2:14)

Pray: Oh Jesus, meek and humble of heart, make our hearts like unto Thine. (Based on Matthew 11:29)

Jesus Institutes the Eucharist
& Establishes the New Covenant

JOHN 6:52-56, 64, 66; LUKE 22:14-15, 19, 20-21

Prayer Intention: Increase of faith.
And the apostles said unto the Lord, "Increase our faith." (Luke 17:5)

Our Father...(Matthew 6:9-13)

1. **Read:** The Jews therefore strove among themselves, saying, "How can this Man give us His flesh to eat?" (John 6:52)
   Pray: Lord, increase our faith! (Luke 17:5)
   Say: Hail Mary, full of grace, the Lord is with thee. Blessed art thou among women, and blessed is the fruit of thy womb, Jesus. (Luke 1:28 & 42)

2. **Read:** Then Jesus said unto them, "Verily, verily, I say unto you, Except ye eat the Flesh of the Son of Man, and drink His Blood, ye have no life in you." (John 6:53)
   Pray: Lord, increase our faith! (Luke 17:5)
   Say: Hail Mary, full of grace, the Lord is with thee. Blessed art thou among women, and blessed is the fruit of thy womb, Jesus. (Luke 1:28 & 42)

3. **Read:** "Whoso eateth My Flesh, and drinketh My Blood, has eternal life; and I will raise him up at the last day." (John 6:54)
   Pray: Lord, increase our faith! (Luke 17:5)
   Say: Hail Mary, full of grace, the Lord is with thee. Blessed art thou among women, and blessed is the fruit of thy womb, Jesus. (Luke 1:28 & 42)

4. **Read:** "For My Flesh is meat indeed, and My Blood is drink indeed." (John 6:55)
   Pray: Lord, increase our faith! (Luke 17:5)

Say: Hail Mary, full of grace, the Lord is with thee. Blessed art thou among women, and blessed is the fruit of thy womb, Jesus. (Luke 1:28 & 42)

5. **Read:** "He that eateth My Flesh, and drinketh My Blood, dwelleth in Me, and I in him." (John 6:56)
   Pray: Lord, increase our faith! (Luke 17:5)
   Say: Hail Mary, full of grace, the Lord is with thee. Blessed art thou among women, and blessed is the fruit of thy womb, Jesus. (Luke 1:28 & 42)

6. **Read:** "But there are some of you that believe not." For Jesus knew from the beginning who they were that believed not, and who should betray Him. (John 6:64)
   Pray: Lord, increase our faith! (Luke 17:5)
   Say: Hail Mary, full of grace, the Lord is with thee. Blessed art thou among women, and blessed is the fruit of thy womb, Jesus. (Luke 1:28 & 42)

7. **Read:** From that time many of His disciples went back, and walked no more with Him. (John 6:66)
   Pray: Lord, increase our faith! (Luke 17:5)
   Say: Hail Mary, full of grace, the Lord is with thee. Blessed art thou among women, and blessed is the fruit of thy womb, Jesus. (Luke 1:28 & 42)

8. **Read:** And when the hour was come, He sat down, and the twelve apostles with Him. And He said unto them, "With desire I have desired to eat this Passover with you before I suffer." (Luke 22:14-15)
   Pray: Lord, increase our faith! (Luke 17:5)
   Say: Hail Mary, full of grace, the Lord is with thee. Blessed art thou among women, and blessed is the fruit of thy womb, Jesus. (Luke 1:28 & 42)

9. **Read:** And He took bread, and gave thanks, and broke it, and gave unto them, saying, "This is My Body which is given for you: this do in remembrance of Me." (Luke 22:19)

Pray: Lord, increase our faith! (Luke 17:5)

Say: Hail Mary, full of grace, the Lord is with thee. Blessed art thou among women, and blessed is the fruit of thy womb, Jesus. (Luke 1:28 & 42)

10. **Read:** Likewise also the cup after supper, saying, "This cup is the new testament in My Blood, which is shed for you. But, behold, the hand of him that betrayeth Me is with Me on the table." (Luke 22:20-21)

    Pray: Lord, increase our faith! (Luke 17:5)

    Say: Hail Mary, full of grace, the Lord is with thee. Blessed art thou among women, and blessed is the fruit of thy womb, Jesus. (Luke 1:28 & 42)

Pray: Glory to God in the highest! (Luke 2:14)

Pray: Oh Jesus, meek and humble of heart, make our hearts like unto Thine. (Based on Matthew 11:29)

CLOSING PRAYER

We give Thee thanks, O Lord God Almighty,
Who is, and was, and is to come.
(Revelation 11:17)

Great and marvelous are Thy works, Lord God
Almighty;
just and true are Thy ways, Thou King of saints.
(Revelation 15:3)

Praise our God, all ye His servants,
and ye that fear Him, both small and great.
(Revelation 19:5)

Amen.
Even so, come, Lord Jesus.
The grace of our Lord Jesus Christ be with you all.
Amen.
(Revelation 22:20-21)

Sorrowful Mysteries

OPENING PRAYER

Oh God, pour out Your Spirit upon all flesh:
on our sons and on our daughters,
and on our young men, and on our old men.

And on Your servants and on Your handmaidens
pour out Your Spirit.
Amen.

(Based on Acts 2:17-18*)*

The Agony of Jesus in the Garden
MATTHEW 26:36-46

Prayer Intention: Conformity to God's will.
"Not every one that saith unto Me, 'Lord, Lord', shall enter into the kingdom of heaven; but he that doeth the will of My Father Who is in heaven." (Matthew 7:21)

Our Father... (Matthew 6:9-13)

1. **Read:** Then cometh Jesus with them unto a place called Gethsemane, and saith unto the disciples, "Sit ye here, while I go and pray yonder." (Matthew 26:36)
   Pray: Father, not My will, but Thine, be done! (Luke 22:42)
   Say: Hail Mary, full of grace, the Lord is with thee. Blessed art thou among women, and blessed is the fruit of thy womb, Jesus. (Luke 1:28 & 42)

2. **Read:** And He took with Him Peter and the two sons of Zebedee, and began to be sorrowful and very heavy. (Matthew 26:37)
   Pray: Father, not My will, but Thine, be done! (Luke 22:42)
   Say: Hail Mary, full of grace, the Lord is with thee. Blessed art thou among women, and blessed is the fruit of thy womb, Jesus. (Luke 1:28 & 42)

3. **Read:** Then saith He unto them, "My soul is exceeding sorrowful, even unto death: tarry ye here, and watch with Me." (Matthew 26:38)
   Pray: Father, not My will, but Thine, be done! (Luke 22:42)
   Say: Hail Mary, full of grace, the Lord is with thee. Blessed art thou among women, and blessed is the fruit of thy womb, Jesus. (Luke 1:28 & 42)

4. **Read:** And He went a little farther, and fell on His face, and prayed, saying, "O My Father, if it be possible, let this cup pass from Me: nevertheless not as I will, but as Thou wilt." (Matthew 26:39)
   Pray: Father, not My will, but Thine, be done! (Luke 22:42)
   Say: Hail Mary, full of grace, the Lord is with thee. Blessed art thou among women, and blessed is the fruit of thy womb, Jesus. (Luke 1:28 & 42)

5. **Read:** And He came unto the disciples, and found them asleep, and said unto Peter, "What, could ye not watch with Me one hour?" (Matthew 26:40)
   Pray: Father, not My will, but Thine, be done! (Luke 22:42)
   Say: Hail Mary, full of grace, the Lord is with thee. Blessed art thou among women, and blessed is the fruit of thy womb, Jesus. (Luke 1:28 & 42)

6. **Read:** "Watch and pray, that ye enter not into temptation: the spirit indeed is willing, but the flesh is weak." (Matthew 26:41)
   Pray: Father, not My will, but Thine, be done! (Luke 22:42)
   Say: Hail Mary, full of grace, the Lord is with thee. Blessed art thou among women, and blessed is the fruit of thy womb, Jesus. (Luke 1:28 & 42)

7. **Read:** He went away again the second time, and prayed, saying, "O My Father, if this cup may not pass away from Me, except I drink it, Thy will be done." (Matthew 26:42)
   Pray: Father, not My will, but Thine, be done! (Luke 22:42)
   Say: Hail Mary, full of grace, the Lord is with thee. Blessed art thou among women, and blessed is the fruit of thy womb, Jesus. (Luke 1:28 & 42)

8. **Read:** And He came and found them asleep again: for their eyes were heavy. (Matthew 26:43)
   Pray: Father, not My will, but Thine, be done! (Luke 22:42)

Say: Hail Mary, full of grace, the Lord is with thee. Blessed art thou among women, and blessed is the fruit of thy womb, Jesus. (Luke 1:28 & 42)

9. **Read:** And He left them, and went away again, and prayed the third time, saying the same words. (Matthew 26:44)
   Pray: Father, not My will, but Thine, be done! (Luke 22:42)
   Say: Hail Mary, full of grace, the Lord is with thee. Blessed art thou among women, and blessed is the fruit of thy womb, Jesus. (Luke 1:28 & 42)

10. **Read:** Then cometh He to His disciples, and saith unto them, "Sleep on now, and take your rest: behold, the hour is at hand, and the Son of man is betrayed into the hands of sinners." (Matthew 26:45-46)
    Pray: Father, not My will, but Thine, be done! (Luke 22:42)
    Say: Hail Mary, full of grace, the Lord is with thee. Blessed art thou among women, and blessed is the fruit of thy womb, Jesus. (Luke 1:28 & 42)

Pray: Glory to God in the highest! (Luke 2:14)

Pray: Oh Jesus, meek and humble of heart, make our hearts like unto Thine. (Based on Matthew 11:29)

The Scourging of Jesus at the Pillar

JOHN 18:28-31, 39-40; 19:1; MATTHEW 27:18, 20, 22;
LUKE 23:14, 16

Prayer Intention: Love of enemies.
"But I say unto you, Love your enemies, bless them that curse you, do good to them that hate you, and pray for them which despitefully use you, and persecute you." (Matthew 5:44)

"For if ye forgive men their trespasses, your heavenly Father will also forgive you." (Matthew 6:14)

Our Father... (Matthew 6:9-13)

1. **Read:** Then led they Jesus from Caiaphas unto the hall of judgment: and it was early. (John 18:28)
   Pray: Father, forgive them; for they know not what they do. (Luke 23:34)
   Say: Hail Mary, full of grace, the Lord is with thee. Blessed art thou among women, and blessed is the fruit of thy womb, Jesus. (Luke 1:28 & 42)

2. **Read:** Pilate then went out unto them, and said, "What accusation bring ye against this Man?" (John 18:29)
   Pray: Father, forgive them; for they know not what they do. (Luke 23:34)
   Say: Hail Mary, full of grace, the Lord is with thee. Blessed art thou among women, and blessed is the fruit of thy womb, Jesus. (Luke 1:28 & 42)

3. **Read:** They answered and said unto him, "If He were not a malefactor, we would not have delivered Him up unto thee." (John 18:30)

Pray: Father, forgive them; for they know not what they do. (Luke 23:34)

Say: Hail Mary, full of grace, the Lord is with thee. Blessed art thou among women, and blessed is the fruit of thy womb, Jesus. (Luke 1:28 & 42)

4. **Read:** Then said Pilate unto them,…"But ye have a custom, that I should release unto you one at the Passover: will ye therefore that I release unto you the King of the Jews?" (John 18:31 & 39)

   Pray: Father, forgive them; for they know not what they do. (Luke 23:34)

   Say: Hail Mary, full of grace, the Lord is with thee. Blessed art thou among women, and blessed is the fruit of thy womb, Jesus. (Luke 1:28 & 42)

5. **Read:** For he knew that for envy they had delivered Him. (Matthew 27:18)

   Pray: Father, forgive them; for they know not what they do. (Luke 23:34)

   Say: Hail Mary, full of grace, the Lord is with thee. Blessed art thou among women, and blessed is the fruit of thy womb, Jesus. (Luke 1:28 & 42)

6. **Read:** But the chief priests and elders persuaded the multitude that they should ask [for] Barabbas, and destroy Jesus. (Matthew 27:20)

   Pray: Father, forgive them; for they know not what they do. (Luke 23:34)

   Say: Hail Mary, full of grace, the Lord is with thee. Blessed art thou among women, and blessed is the fruit of thy womb, Jesus. (Luke 1:28 & 42)

7. **Read:** Then cried they all again, saying, "Not this Man, but Barabbas." Now Barabbas was a robber. (John 18:40)

   Pray: Father, forgive them; for they know not what they do. (Luke 23:34)

Say: Hail Mary, full of grace, the Lord is with thee. Blessed art thou among women, and blessed is the fruit of thy womb, Jesus. (Luke 1:28 & 42)

8. **Read:** Pilate said unto them, "What shall I do then with Jesus which is called Christ?" They all said unto him, "Let Him be crucified." (Matthew 27:22)
   Pray: Father, forgive them; for they know not what they do. (Luke 23:34)
   Say: Hail Mary, full of grace, the Lord is with thee. Blessed art thou among women, and blessed is the fruit of thy womb, Jesus. (Luke 1:28 & 42)

9. **Read:** [Pilate] said unto them, "Ye have brought this Man unto me, as one that perverteth the people: and, behold, I, having examined Him before you, have found no fault in this Man touching those things whereof ye accuse Him:....I will therefore chastise Him, and release Him." (Luke 23:14 & 16)
   Pray: Father, forgive them; for they know not what they do. (Luke 23:34)
   Say: Hail Mary, full of grace, the Lord is with thee. Blessed art thou among women, and blessed is the fruit of thy womb, Jesus. (Luke 1:28 & 42)

10. **Read:** Then Pilate therefore took Jesus, and scourged Him. (John 19:1)
    Pray: Father, forgive them; for they know not what they do. (Luke 23:34)
    Say: Hail Mary, full of grace, the Lord is with thee. Blessed art thou among women, and blessed is the fruit of thy womb, Jesus. (Luke 1:28 & 42)

Pray: Glory to God in the highest! (Luke 2:14)

Pray: Oh Jesus, meek and humble of heart, make our hearts like unto Thine. (Based on Matthew 11:29)

The Crowning of Jesus with Thorns
Matthew 27:27-28, 30; John 19:2-5, 14-16

Prayer Intention: Reverence for the Kingship of Jesus.
And set up over His head His accusation written, This Is Jesus The King Of The Jews. (Matthew 27:37)

Our Father... (Matthew 6:9-13)

1. **Read:** Then the soldiers of the governor took Jesus into the common hall, and gathered unto Him the whole band of soldiers. (Matthew 27:27)
   Pray: Jesus, Thou art the King of Israel; have mercy on me. (John 1:49 & Mark 10:47)
   Say: Hail Mary, full of grace, the Lord is with thee. Blessed art thou among women, and blessed is the fruit of thy womb, Jesus. (Luke 1:28 & 42)

2. **Read:** And they stripped Him, and put on Him a scarlet robe. (Matthew 27:28)
   Pray: Jesus, Thou art the King of Israel; have mercy on me. (John 1:49 & Mark 10:47)
   Say: Hail Mary, full of grace, the Lord is with thee. Blessed art thou among women, and blessed is the fruit of thy womb, Jesus. (Luke 1:28 & 42)

3. **Read:** And the soldiers platted a crown of thorns, and put it on His head. (John 19:2)
   Pray: Jesus, Thou art the King of Israel, have mercy on me. (John 1:49 & Mark 10:47)
   Say: Hail Mary, full of grace, the Lord is with thee. Blessed art thou among women, and blessed is the fruit of thy womb, Jesus. (Luke 1:28 & 42)

4. **Read:** And said, "Hail, King of the Jews!" and they smote Him with their hands. (John 19:3)
   Pray: Jesus, Thou art the King of Israel; have mercy on me. (John 1:49 & Mark 10:47)
   Say: Hail Mary, full of grace, the Lord is with thee. Blessed art thou among women, and blessed is the fruit of thy womb, Jesus. (Luke 1:28 & 42)

5. **Read:** And they spit upon Him, and took the reed, and smote Him on the head. (Matthew 27:30)
   Pray: Jesus, Thou art the King of Israel; have mercy on me. (John 1:49 & Mark 10:47)
   Say: Hail Mary, full of grace, the Lord is with thee. Blessed art thou among women, and blessed is the fruit of thy womb, Jesus. (Luke 1:28 & 42)

6. **Read:** Pilate therefore went forth again, and said unto them, "Behold, I bring Him forth to you, that ye may know that I find no fault in Him." (John 19:4)
   Pray: Jesus, Thou art the King of Israel; have mercy on me. (John 1:49 & Mark 10:47)
   Say: Hail Mary, full of grace, the Lord is with thee. Blessed art thou among women, and blessed is the fruit of thy womb, Jesus. (Luke 1:28 & 42)

7. **Read:** Then came Jesus forth, wearing the crown of thorns, and the purple robe. And Pilate said unto them, "Behold the Man!" (John 19:5)
   Pray: Jesus, Thou art the King of Israel; have mercy on me. (John 1:49 & Mark 10:47)
   Say: Hail Mary, full of grace, the Lord is with thee. Blessed art thou among women, and blessed is the fruit of thy womb, Jesus. (Luke 1:28 & 42)

8. **Read:** And it was the preparation of the Passover, and about the sixth hour: and he said unto the Jews, "Behold your King!" (John 19:14)

Pray: Jesus, Thou art the King of Israel; have mercy on me. (John 1:49 & Mark 10:47)

Say: Hail Mary, full of grace, the Lord is with thee. Blessed art thou among women, and blessed is the fruit of thy womb, Jesus. (Luke 1:28 & 42)

9. **Read:** But they cried out, "Away with Him, away with Him, crucify Him." Pilate said unto them, "Shall I crucify your King?" The chief priests answered, "We have no king but Caesar." (John 19:15)

    Pray: Jesus, Thou art the King of Israel; have mercy on me. (John 1:49 & Mark 10:47)

    Say: Hail Mary, full of grace, the Lord is with thee. Blessed art thou among women, and blessed is the fruit of thy womb, Jesus. (Luke 1:28 & 42)

10. **Read:** Then [Pilot] delivered [Jesus] therefore unto them to be crucified. And they took Jesus, and led Him away. (John 19:16)

    Pray: Jesus, Thou art the King of Israel; have mercy on me. (John 1:49 & Mark 10:47)

    Say: Hail Mary, full of grace, the Lord is with thee. Blessed art thou among women, and blessed is the fruit of thy womb, Jesus. (Luke 1:28 & 42)

Pray: Glory to God in the highest! (Luke 2:14)

Pray: Oh Jesus, meek and humble of heart, make our hearts like unto Thine. (Based on Matthew 11:29)

Jesus Carries His Cross
LUKE 9:23; 23:26-32; JOHN 19:17

Prayer Intention: Self-denial; to take up our cross and follow Jesus.
And when He had called the people unto Him with His disciples also, He said unto them, "Whosoever will come after Me, let him deny himself, and take up his cross, and follow Me." (Mark 8:34. Also, Matthew 10:38; Luke 9:23; 14:27)

Our Father... (Matthew 6:9-13)

1. **Read:** And He said to them all, "If any man will come after Me, let him deny himself, and take up his cross daily, and follow Me." (Luke 9:23)
    Pray: Lamb of God, which taketh away the sin of the world, be merciful to me, a sinner. (John 1:29 & Luke 18:13)
    Say: Hail Mary, full of grace, the Lord is with thee. Blessed art thou among women, and blessed is the fruit of thy womb, Jesus. (Luke 1:28 & 42)

2. **Read:** And He bearing His cross went forth into a place called the place of a skull, which is called in the Hebrew Golgotha. (John 19:17)
    Pray: Lamb of God, which taketh away the sin of the world, be merciful to me, a sinner. (John 1:29 & Luke 18:13)
    Say: Hail Mary, full of grace, the Lord is with thee. Blessed art thou among women, and blessed is the fruit of thy womb, Jesus. (Luke 1:28 & 42)

3. **Read:** And as they led Him away, they laid hold upon one Simon, a Cyrenian, coming out of the country, and on him they laid the cross, that he might bear it after Jesus. (Luke 23:26)

Pray: Lamb of God, which taketh away the sin of the world, be merciful to me, a sinner. (John 1:29 & Luke 18:13)
Say: Hail Mary, full of grace, the Lord is with thee. Blessed art thou among women, and blessed is the fruit of thy womb, Jesus. (Luke 1:28 & 42)

4. **Read:** And there followed Him a great company of people, and of women, which also bewailed and lamented Him. (Luke 23:27)
Pray: Lamb of God, which taketh away the sin of the world, be merciful to me, a sinner. (John 1:29 & Luke 18:13)
Say: Hail Mary, full of grace, the Lord is with thee. Blessed art thou among women, and blessed is the fruit of thy womb, Jesus. (Luke 1:28 & 42)

5. **Read:** But Jesus turning unto them said, "Daughters of Jerusalem, weep not for Me," (Luke 23:28a)
Pray: Lamb of God, which taketh away the sin of the world, be merciful to me, a sinner. (John 1:29 & Luke 18:13)
Say: Hail Mary, full of grace, the Lord is with thee. Blessed art thou among women, and blessed is the fruit of thy womb, Jesus. (Luke 1:28 & 42)

6. **Read:** "...but weep for yourselves, and for your children." (Luke 23:28b)
Pray: Lamb of God, which taketh away the sin of the world, be merciful to me, a sinner. (John 1:29 & Luke 18:13)
Say: Hail Mary, full of grace, the Lord is with thee. Blessed art thou among women, and blessed is the fruit of thy womb, Jesus. (Luke 1:28 & 42)

7. **Read:** "For, behold, the days are coming, in which they shall say, 'Blessed are the barren, and the wombs that never bare, and the paps which never gave suck.'" (Luke 23:29)
Pray: Lamb of God, which taketh away the sin of the world, be merciful to me, a sinner. (John 1:29 & Luke 18:13)

Say: Hail Mary, full of grace, the Lord is with thee. Blessed art thou among women, and blessed is the fruit of thy womb, Jesus. (Luke 1:28 & 42)

8. **Read:** "Then shall they begin to say to the mountains, 'Fall on us;' and to the hills, 'Cover us.'" (Luke 23:30)
   Pray: Lamb of God, which taketh away the sin of the world, be merciful to me, a sinner. (John 1:29 & Luke 18:13)
   Say: Hail Mary, full of grace, the Lord is with thee. Blessed art thou among women, and blessed is the fruit of thy womb, Jesus. (Luke 1:28 & 42)

9. **Read:** "For if they do these things in a green tree, what shall be done in the dry?" (Luke 23:31)
   Pray: Lamb of God, which taketh away the sin of the world, be merciful to me, a sinner. (John 1:29 & Luke 18:13)
   Say: Hail Mary, full of grace, the Lord is with thee. Blessed art thou among women, and blessed is the fruit of thy womb, Jesus. (Luke 1:28 & 42)

10. **Read:** And there were also two other, malefactors, led with Him to be put to death. (Luke 23:32)
    Pray: Lamb of God, which taketh away the sin of the world, be merciful to me, a sinner. (John 1:29 & Luke 18:13)
    Say: Hail Mary, full of grace, the Lord is with thee. Blessed art thou among women, and blessed is the fruit of thy womb, Jesus. (Luke 1:28 & 42)

Pray: Glory to God in the highest! (Luke 2:14)

Pray: Oh Jesus, meek and humble of heart, make our hearts like unto Thine. (Based on Matthew 11:29)

The Crucifixion and Death of Jesus
Luke 23:33, 39-43, 46; John 19:26-27; Mark 15:39

Prayer Intention: Conversion of sinners.
"I came not to call the righteous, but sinners to repentance."
(Luke 5:32)

Our Father... (Matthew 6:9-13)

1. **Read:** And when they were come to the place, which is called Calvary, there they crucified Him, and the malefactors, one on the right hand, and the other on the left. (Luke 23:33)
   Pray: Jesus, Lord, remember me when Thou comest into Thy kingdom. (Luke 23:42)
   Say: Hail Mary, full of grace, the Lord is with thee. Blessed art thou among women, and blessed is the fruit of thy womb, Jesus. (Luke 1:28 & 42)

2. **Read:** And one of the malefactors which were hanged railed on Him, saying, "If Thou be Christ, save Thyself and us." (Luke 23:39)
   Pray: Jesus, Lord, remember me when Thou comest into Thy kingdom. (Luke 23:42)
   Say: Hail Mary, full of grace, the Lord is with thee. Blessed art thou among women, and blessed is the fruit of thy womb, Jesus. (Luke 1:28 & 42)

3. **Read:** But the other answering rebuked him, saying, "Dost not thou fear God, seeing thou art in the same condemnation?" (Luke 23:40)
   Pray: Jesus, Lord, remember me when Thou comest into Thy kingdom. (Luke 23:42)

Say: Hail Mary, full of grace, the Lord is with thee. Blessed art thou among women, and blessed is the fruit of thy womb, Jesus. (Luke 1:28 & 42)

4. **Read:** "And we indeed justly; for we receive the due reward of our deeds: but this Man hath done nothing amiss." (Luke 23:41)

   Pray: Jesus, Lord, remember me when Thou comest into Thy kingdom. (Luke 23:42)

   Say: Hail Mary, full of grace, the Lord is with thee. Blessed art thou among women, and blessed is the fruit of thy womb, Jesus. (Luke 1:28 & 42)

5. **Read:** And he said unto Jesus, "Lord, remember me when Thou comest into Thy kingdom." (Luke 23:42)

   Pray: Jesus, Lord, remember me when Thou comest into Thy kingdom. (Luke 23:42)

   Say: Hail Mary, full of grace, the Lord is with thee. Blessed art thou among women, and blessed is the fruit of thy womb, Jesus. (Luke 1:28 & 42)

6. **Read:** And Jesus said unto him, "Verily I say unto thee, Today shalt thou be with Me in paradise." (Luke 23:43)

   Pray: Jesus, Lord, remember me when Thou comest into Thy kingdom. (Luke 23:42)

   Say: Hail Mary, full of grace, the Lord is with thee. Blessed art thou among women, and blessed is the fruit of thy womb, Jesus. (Luke 1:28 & 42)

7. **Read:** When Jesus therefore saw His mother, and the disciple standing by, whom He loved, He said unto His mother, "Woman, behold thy son!" (John 19:26)

   Pray: Jesus, Lord, remember me when Thou comest into Thy kingdom. (Luke 23:42)

   Say: Hail Mary, full of grace, the Lord is with thee. Blessed art thou among women, and blessed is the fruit of thy womb, Jesus. (Luke 1:28 & 42)

8. **Read:** Then said He to the disciple, "Behold thy mother!" And from that hour that disciple took her unto his own home. (John 19:27)
   Pray: Jesus, Lord, remember me when Thou comest into Thy kingdom. (Luke 23:42)
   Say: Hail Mary, full of grace, the Lord is with thee. Blessed art thou among women, and blessed is the fruit of thy womb, Jesus. (Luke 1:28 & 42)

9. **Read:** And when Jesus had cried with a loud voice, He said, "Father, into Thy hands I commend My spirit:" and having said thus, He gave up the ghost. (Luke 23:46)
   Pray: Jesus, Lord, remember me when Thou comest into Thy kingdom. (Luke 23:42)
   Say: Hail Mary, full of grace, the Lord is with thee. Blessed art thou among women, and blessed is the fruit of thy womb, Jesus. (Luke 1:28 & 42)

10. **Read:** And when the centurion, which stood over against Him, saw that He so cried out, and gave up the ghost, he said, "Truly this Man was the Son of God." (Mark 15:39)
    Pray: Jesus, Lord, remember me when Thou comest into Thy kingdom. (Luke 23:42)
    Say: Hail Mary, full of grace, the Lord is with thee. Blessed art thou among women, and blessed is the fruit of thy womb, Jesus. (Luke 1:28 & 42)

Pray: Glory to God in the highest! (Luke 2:14)

Pray: Oh Jesus, meek and humble of heart, make our hearts like unto Thine. (Based on Matthew 11:29)

CLOSING PRAYER

We give Thee thanks, O Lord God Almighty,
Who is, and was, and is to come.
(Revelation 11:17)

Great and marvelous are Thy works, Lord God
Almighty;
just and true are Thy ways, Thou King of saints.
(Revelation 15:3)

Praise our God, all ye His servants,
and ye that fear Him, both small and great.
(Revelation 19:5)

Amen.
Even so, come, Lord Jesus.
The grace of our Lord Jesus Christ be with you all.
Amen.
(Revelation 22:20-21)

Glorious Mysteries

OPENING PRAYER

Oh God, pour out Your Spirit upon all flesh:
on our sons and on our daughters,
and on our young men, and on our old men.

And on Your servants and on Your handmaidens
pour out Your Spirit.
Amen.

(Based on Acts 2:17-18*)*

The Resurrection of Jesus from the Dead

MATTHEW 28:1-2, 5-9; JOHN 20:19-20, 22-23

Prayer Intention: Love of God and fervor in His service.
"And thou shalt love the Lord thy God with all thy heart, and with all thy soul, and with all thy mind, and with all thy strength." (Mark 12:30)

"If ye love Me, keep My commandments." (John 14:15)

Our Father... (Matthew 6:9-13)

1. **Read:** In the end of the Sabbath, as it began to dawn toward the first day of the week, came Mary Magdalene and the other Mary to see the sepulcher. (Matthew 28:1)
   Pray: My Lord and my God! I love Thee! (John 20:28; 21:15-17)
   Say: Hail Mary, full of grace, the Lord is with thee. Blessed art thou among women, and blessed is the fruit of thy womb, Jesus. (Luke 1:28 & 42)

2. **Read:** And, behold, there was a great earthquake: for the angel of the Lord descended from heaven, and came and rolled back the stone from the door, and sat upon it. (Matthew 28:2)
   Pray: My Lord and my God! I love Thee! (John 20:28; 21:15-17)
   Say: Hail Mary, full of grace, the Lord is with thee. Blessed art thou among women, and blessed is the fruit of thy womb, Jesus. (Luke 1:28 & 42)

3. **Read:** And the angel answered and said unto the women, "Fear not ye: for I know that ye seek Jesus, Who was crucified." (Matthew 28:5)
   Pray: My Lord and my God! I love Thee! (John 20:28; 21:15-17)

Say: Hail Mary, full of grace, the Lord is with thee. Blessed art thou among women, and blessed is the fruit of thy womb, Jesus. (Luke 1:28 & 42)

4. **Read:** "He is not here: for He is risen, as He said. Come, see the place where the Lord lay." (Matthew 28:6)
   Pray: My Lord and my God! I love Thee! (John 20:28; 21:15-17)
   Say: Hail Mary, full of grace, the Lord is with thee. Blessed art thou among women, and blessed is the fruit of thy womb, Jesus. (Luke 1:28 & 42)

5. **Read:** "And go quickly, and tell His disciples that He is risen from the dead; and, behold, He goeth before you into Galilee; there shall ye see Him: lo, I have told you." (Matthew 28:7)
   Pray: My Lord and my God! I love Thee! (John 20:28; 21:15-17)
   Say: Hail Mary, full of grace, the Lord is with thee. Blessed art thou among women, and blessed is the fruit of thy womb, Jesus. (Luke 1:28 & 42)

6. **Read:** And they departed quickly from the sepulcher with fear and great joy; and did run to bring His disciples word. (Matthew 28:8)
   Pray: My Lord and my God! I love Thee! (John 20:28; 21:15-17)
   Say: Hail Mary, full of grace, the Lord is with thee. Blessed art thou among women, and blessed is the fruit of thy womb, Jesus. (Luke 1:28 & 42)

7. **Read:** And as they went to tell His disciples, behold, Jesus met them, saying, "All hail." And they came and held Him by the feet, and worshipped Him. (Matthew 28:9)
   Pray: My Lord and my God! I love Thee! (John 20:28; 21:15-17)
   Say: Hail Mary, full of grace, the Lord is with thee. Blessed art thou among women, and blessed is the fruit of thy womb, Jesus. (Luke 1:28 & 42)

8. **Read:** Then the same day at evening, being the first day of the week, when the doors were shut where the disciples were assembled for fear of the Jews, came Jesus and stood

in the midst, and saith unto them, "Peace be unto you."
(John 20:19)
Pray: My Lord and my God! I love Thee! (John 20:28; 21:15-17)
Say: Hail Mary, full of grace, the Lord is with thee. Blessed
art thou among women, and blessed is the fruit of thy
womb, Jesus. (Luke 1:28 & 42)

9. **Read:** And when He had so said, He showed unto them His
    hands and His side. Then were the disciples glad, when they
    saw the Lord. (John 20:20)
    Pray: My Lord and my God! I love Thee! (John 20:28; 21:15-17)
    Say: Hail Mary, full of grace, the Lord is with thee. Blessed
    art thou among women, and blessed is the fruit of thy
    womb, Jesus. (Luke 1:28 & 42)

10. **Read:** And when He had said this, He breathed on them, and
    saith unto them, "Receive ye the Holy Ghost: Whose soever
    sins ye remit, they are remitted unto them; and whose
    soever sins ye retain, they are retained." (John 20:22-23)
    Pray: My Lord and my God! I love Thee! (John 20:28; 21:15-17)
    Say: Hail Mary, full of grace, the Lord is with thee. Blessed
    art thou among women, and blessed is the fruit of thy
    womb, Jesus. (Luke 1:28 & 42)

Pray: Glory to God in the highest! (Luke 2:14)

Pray: Oh Jesus, meek and humble of heart, make our hearts
like unto Thine. (Based on Matthew 11:29)

The Ascension of Jesus into Heaven
MATTHEW 28:16, 18-19; MARK 16:16; ACTS 1:8-14

Prayer Intention: Longing for heaven, our true home.
"In My Father's house are many mansions: if it were not so, I would have told you. I go to prepare a place for you. And if I go and prepare a place for you, I will come again, and receive you unto Myself; that where I am, there ye may be also." (John 14:2-3)

Our Father... (Matthew 6:9-13)

1. **Read:** Then the eleven disciples went away into Galilee, into a mountain where Jesus had appointed them. (Matthew 28:16)
   Pray: Lord Jesus Christ, to You be honor and power everlasting. Amen. (1 Timothy 6:16)
   Say: Hail Mary, full of grace, the Lord is with thee. Blessed art thou among women, and blessed is the fruit of thy womb, Jesus. (Luke 1:28 & 42)

2. **Read:** And Jesus came and spoke unto them, saying, "All power is given unto Me in heaven and in earth." (Matthew 28:18)
   Pray: Lord Jesus Christ, to You be honor and power everlasting. Amen. (1 Timothy 6:16)
   Say: Hail Mary, full of grace, the Lord is with thee. Blessed art thou among women, and blessed is the fruit of thy womb, Jesus. (Luke 1:28 & 42)

3. **Read:** "Go ye therefore, and teach all nations, baptizing them in the Name of the Father, and of the Son, and of the Holy Ghost." (Matthew 28:19)
   Pray: Lord Jesus Christ, to You be honor and power everlasting. Amen. (1 Timothy 6:16)

Say: Hail Mary, full of grace, the Lord is with thee. Blessed art thou among women, and blessed is the fruit of thy womb, Jesus. (Luke 1:28 & 42)

4. **Read:** "He that believeth and is baptized shall be saved; but he that believeth not shall be damned." (Mark 16:16)

   Pray: Lord Jesus Christ, to You be honor and power everlasting. Amen. (1 Timothy 6:16)

   Say: Hail Mary, full of grace, the Lord is with thee. Blessed art thou among women, and blessed is the fruit of thy womb, Jesus. (Luke 1:28 & 42)

5. **Read:** "But ye shall receive power, after...the Holy Ghost is come upon you: and ye shall be witnesses unto Me both in Jerusalem, and in all Judaea, and in Samaria, and unto the uttermost part of the earth." (Acts 1:8)

   Pray: Lord Jesus Christ, to You be honor and power everlasting. Amen. (1 Timothy 6:16)

   Say: Hail Mary, full of grace, the Lord is with thee. Blessed art thou among women, and blessed is the fruit of thy womb, Jesus. (Luke 1:28 & 42)

6. **Read:** And when He had spoken these things, while they beheld, He was taken up; and a cloud received Him out of their sight. (Acts 1:9)

   Pray: Lord Jesus Christ, to You be honor and power everlasting. Amen. (1 Timothy 6:16)

   Say: Hail Mary, full of grace, the Lord is with thee. Blessed art thou among women, and blessed is the fruit of thy womb, Jesus. (Luke 1:28 & 42)

7. **Read:** And while they looked steadfastly toward heaven as He went up, behold, two men stood by them in white apparel. (Acts 1:10)

   Pray: Lord Jesus Christ, to You be honor and power everlasting. Amen. (1 Timothy 6:16)

Say: Hail Mary, full of grace, the Lord is with thee. Blessed art thou among women, and blessed is the fruit of thy womb, Jesus. (Luke 1:28 & 42)

8. **Read:** Which also said, "Ye men of Galilee, why stand ye gazing up into heaven? This same Jesus, which is taken up from you into heaven, shall so come in like manner as ye have seen Him go into heaven." (Acts 1:11)
   Pray: Lord Jesus Christ, to You be honor and power everlasting. Amen. (1 Timothy 6:16)
   Say: Hail Mary, full of grace, the Lord is with thee. Blessed art thou among women, and blessed is the fruit of thy womb, Jesus. (Luke 1:28 & 42)

9. **Read:** Then returned they unto Jerusalem from the mount called Olivet, which is from Jerusalem a Sabbath day's journey. (Acts 1:12)
   Pray: Lord Jesus Christ, to You be honor and power everlasting. Amen. (1 Timothy 6:16)
   Say: Hail Mary, full of grace, the Lord is with thee. Blessed art thou among women, and blessed is the fruit of thy womb, Jesus. (Luke 1:28 & 42)

10. **Read:** And when they were come in, they went up into an upper room...These all continued with one accord in prayer and supplication, with the women, and Mary the mother of Jesus, and with His brethren. (Acts 1:13-14)
    Pray: Lord Jesus Christ, to You be honor and power everlasting. Amen. (1 Timothy 6:16)
    Say: Hail Mary, full of grace, the Lord is with thee. Blessed art thou among women, and blessed is the fruit of thy womb, Jesus. (Luke 1:28 & 42)

Pray: Glory to God in the highest! (Luke 2:14)

Pray: Oh Jesus, meek and humble of heart, make our hearts like unto Thine. (Based on Matthew 11:29)

The Descent of the Holy Spirit
ACTS 2:1-6, 38-39, 41-42

Prayer Intention: Out-pouring of the Holy Spirit.
"And it shall come to pass in the last days, saith God, I will pour out of My Spirit upon all flesh." (Acts 2:17)

Our Father... (Matthew 6:9-13)

1. **Read:** And when the day of Pentecost was fully come, they were all with one accord in one place. (Acts 2:1)
    Pray: Holy Spirit, teach us all things and remind us of everything Jesus has said. (Based on John 14:26)
    Say: Hail Mary, full of grace, the Lord is with thee. Blessed art thou among women, and blessed is the fruit of thy womb, Jesus. (Luke 1:28 & 42)

2. **Read:** And suddenly there came a sound from heaven as of a rushing mighty wind, and it filled all the house where they were sitting. (Acts 2:2)
    Pray: Holy Spirit, teach us all things and remind us of everything Jesus has said. (Based on John 14:26)
    Say: Hail Mary, full of grace, the Lord is with thee. Blessed art thou among women, and blessed is the fruit of thy womb, Jesus. (Luke 1:28 & 42)

3. **Read:** And there appeared unto them cloven tongues like as of fire, and it sat upon each of them. (Acts 2:3)
    Pray: Holy Spirit, teach us all things and remind us of everything Jesus has said. (Based on John 14:26)
    Say: Hail Mary, full of grace, the Lord is with thee. Blessed art thou among women, and blessed is the fruit of thy womb, Jesus. (Luke 1:28 & 42)

4. **Read:** And they were all filled with the Holy Ghost, and began to speak with other tongues, as the Spirit gave them utterance. (Acts 2:4)
   Pray: Holy Spirit, teach us all things and remind us of everything Jesus has said. (Based on John 14:26)
   Say: Hail Mary, full of grace, the Lord is with thee. Blessed art thou among women, and blessed is the fruit of thy womb, Jesus. (Luke 1:28 & 42)

5. **Read:** And there were dwelling at Jerusalem Jews, devout men, out of every nation under heaven. (Acts 2:5)
   Pray: Holy Spirit, teach us all things and remind us of everything Jesus has said. (Based on John 14:26)
   Say: Hail Mary, full of grace, the Lord is with thee. Blessed art thou among women, and blessed is the fruit of thy womb, Jesus. (Luke 1:28 & 42)

6. **Read:** Now when this was noised abroad, the multitude came together, and were confounded, because...every man heard them speak in his own language. (Acts 2:6)
   Pray: Holy Spirit, teach us all things and remind us of everything Jesus has said. (Based on John 14:26)
   Say: Hail Mary, full of grace, the Lord is with thee. Blessed art thou among women, and blessed is the fruit of thy womb, Jesus. (Luke 1:28 & 42)

7. **Read:** Then Peter said unto them, "Repent, and be baptized every one of you in the Name of Jesus Christ for the remission of sins, and ye shall receive the gift of the Holy Ghost." (Acts 2:38)
   Pray: Holy Spirit, teach us all things and remind us of everything Jesus has said. (Based on John 14:26)
   Say: Hail Mary, full of grace, the Lord is with thee. Blessed art thou among women, and blessed is the fruit of thy womb, Jesus. (Luke 1:28 & 42)

8. **Read:** "For the promise is unto you, and to your children, and to all that are afar off, even as many as the Lord our God shall call." (Acts 2:39)

   Pray: Holy Spirit, teach us all things and remind us of everything Jesus has said. (Based on John 14:26)

   Say: Hail Mary, full of grace, the Lord is with thee. Blessed art thou among women, and blessed is the fruit of thy womb, Jesus. (Luke 1:28 & 42)

9. **Read:** Then they that gladly received his word were baptized: and the same day there were added unto them about three thousand souls. (Acts 2:41)

   Pray: Holy Spirit, teach us all things and remind us of everything Jesus has said. (Based on John 14:26)

   Say: Hail Mary, full of grace, the Lord is with thee. Blessed art thou among women, and blessed is the fruit of thy womb, Jesus. (Luke 1:28 & 42)

10. **Read:** And they continued steadfastly in the apostles' doctrine and fellowship, and in breaking of bread, and in prayers. (Acts 2:42)

    Pray: Holy Spirit, teach us all things and remind us of everything Jesus has said. (Based on John 14:26)

    Say: Hail Mary, full of grace, the Lord is with thee. Blessed art thou among women, and blessed is the fruit of thy womb, Jesus. (Luke 1:28 & 42)

Pray: Glory to God in the highest! (Luke 2:14)

Pray: Oh Jesus, meek and humble of heart, make our hearts like unto Thine. (Based on Matthew 11:29)

The Woman Clothed with the Sun

GENESIS 3:14-15; REVELATION 11:19; 12:1-6A, 9, 17

Prayer Intention: Grace to keep God's commandments and bear witness to Jesus.

And the dragon was wroth with the woman, and went to make war with the remnant of her seed, which keep the commandments of God, and have the testimony of Jesus Christ. (Revelation 12:17)

Our Father... (Matthew 6:9-13)

1. **Read:** And the Lord God said unto the serpent..."And I will put enmity between thee and the woman, and between thy seed and her seed; it shall bruise thy head, and thou shalt bruise his heel." (Genesis 3:14-15)
   Pray: He that is mighty hath done to me great things; and holy is His name. (Luke 1:49)
   Say: Hail Mary, full of grace, the Lord is with thee. Blessed art thou among women, and blessed is the fruit of thy womb, Jesus. (Luke 1:28 & 42)

2. **Read:** And the temple of God was opened in heaven, and there was seen in His temple the ark of His testament: and there were lightnings, and voices, and thunderings, and an earthquake, and great hail. (Revelation 11:19)
   Pray: He that is mighty hath done to me great things; and holy is His name. (Luke 1:49)
   Say: Hail Mary, full of grace, the Lord is with thee. Blessed art thou among women, and blessed is the fruit of thy womb, Jesus. (Luke 1:28 & 42)

3. **Read:** And there appeared a great wonder in heaven; a woman clothed with the sun, and the moon under her feet, and upon her head a crown of twelve stars. (Revelation 12:1)

Pray: He that is mighty hath done to me great things; and holy is His name. (Luke 1:49)
Say: Hail Mary, full of grace, the Lord is with thee. Blessed art thou among women, and blessed is the fruit of thy womb, Jesus. (Luke 1:28 & 42)

4. **Read:** And she being with Child cried, travailing in birth, and pained to be delivered. (Revelation 12:2)
Pray: He that is mighty hath done to me great things; and holy is His name. (Luke 1:49)
Say: Hail Mary, full of grace, the Lord is with thee. Blessed art thou among women, and blessed is the fruit of thy womb, Jesus. (Luke 1:28 & 42)

5. **Read:** And there appeared another wonder in heaven; and behold a great red dragon, having seven heads and ten horns, and seven crowns upon his heads. (Revelation 12:3)
Pray: He that is mighty hath done to me great things; and holy is His name. (Luke 1:49)
Say: Hail Mary, full of grace, the Lord is with thee. Blessed art thou among women, and blessed is the fruit of thy womb, Jesus. (Luke 1:28 & 42)

6. **Read:** And his tail drew the third part of the stars of heaven, and did cast them to the earth. And the dragon stood before the woman which was ready to be delivered, for to devour her Child as soon as it was born. (Revelation 12:4)
Pray: He that is mighty hath done to me great things; and holy is His name. (Luke 1:49)
Say: Hail Mary, full of grace, the Lord is with thee. Blessed art thou among women, and blessed is the fruit of thy womb, Jesus. (Luke 1:28 & 42)

7. **Read:** And she brought forth a Man Child, Who was to rule all nations with a rod of iron: and her Child was caught up unto God, and to His throne. (Revelation 12:5)

Pray: He that is mighty hath done to me great things; and holy is His name. (Luke 1:49)

Say: Hail Mary, full of grace, the Lord is with thee. Blessed art thou among women, and blessed is the fruit of thy womb, Jesus. (Luke 1:28 & 42)

8. **Read:** And the woman fled into the wilderness, where she had a place prepared of God. (Revelation 12:6a)

    Pray: He that is mighty hath done to me great things; and holy is His name. (Luke 1:49)

    Say: Hail Mary, full of grace, the Lord is with thee. Blessed art thou among women, and blessed is the fruit of thy womb, Jesus. (Luke 1:28 & 42)

9. **Read:** And the great dragon was cast out, that old serpent, called the Devil, and Satan, which deceiveth the whole world: he was cast out into the earth, and his angels were cast out with him. (Revelation 12:9)

    Pray: He that is mighty hath done to me great things; and holy is His name. (Luke 1:49)

    Say: Hail Mary, full of grace, the Lord is with thee. Blessed art thou among women, and blessed is the fruit of thy womb, Jesus. (Luke 1:28 & 42)

10. **Read:** And the dragon was wroth with the woman, and went to make war with the remnant of her seed, which keep the commandments of God, and have the testimony of Jesus Christ. (Revelation 12:17)

    Pray: He that is mighty hath done to me great things; and holy is His name. (Luke 1:49)

    Say: Hail Mary, full of grace, the Lord is with thee. Blessed art thou among women, and blessed is the fruit of thy womb, Jesus. (Luke 1:28 & 42)

Pray: Glory to God in the highest! (Luke 2:14)

Pray: Oh Jesus, meek and humble of heart, make our hearts like unto Thine. (Based on Matthew 11:29)

The Heavenly Jerusalem

REVELATION 21:1-2, 9-12, 14, 22-23, 26-27

Prayer Intention: Final perseverance.

"And ye shall be hated of all men for My Name's sake: but he that shall endure unto the end, the same shall be saved." (Mark 13:13)

Our Father... (Matthew 6:9-13)

1. **Read:** And I saw a new heaven and a new earth: for the first heaven and the first earth were passed away; and there was no more sea. (Revelation 21:1)
   Pray: Amen, come Lord Jesus! (Revelation 22:20)
   Say: Hail Mary, full of grace, the Lord is with thee. Blessed art thou among women, and blessed is the fruit of thy womb, Jesus. (Luke 1:28 & 42)

2. **Read:** And I, John, saw the holy city, new Jerusalem, coming down from God out of heaven, prepared as a bride adorned for her husband. (Revelation 21:2)
   Pray: Amen, come Lord Jesus! (Revelation 22:20)
   Say: Hail Mary, full of grace, the Lord is with thee. Blessed art thou among women, and blessed is the fruit of thy womb, Jesus. (Luke 1:28 & 42)

3. **Read:** And there came unto me one of the seven angels which had the seven vials full of the seven last plagues, and talked with me, saying, "Come hither, I will show thee the bride, the Lamb's wife." (Revelation 21:9)
   Pray: Amen, come Lord Jesus! (Revelation 22:20)
   Say: Hail Mary, full of grace, the Lord is with thee. Blessed art thou among women, and blessed is the fruit of thy womb, Jesus. (Luke 1:28 & 42)

4. **Read:** And he carried me away in the spirit to a great and high mountain, and showed me that great city, the holy Jerusalem, descending out of heaven from God. (Revelation 21:10)

   Pray: Amen, come Lord Jesus! (Revelation 22:20)

   Say: Hail Mary, full of grace, the Lord is with thee. Blessed art thou among women, and blessed is the fruit of thy womb, Jesus. (Luke 1:28 & 42)

5. **Read:** Having the glory of God: and her light was like unto a stone most precious, even like a jasper stone, clear as crystal. (Revelation 21:11)

   Pray: Amen, come Lord Jesus! (Revelation 22:20)

   Say: Hail Mary, full of grace, the Lord is with thee. Blessed art thou among women, and blessed is the fruit of thy womb, Jesus. (Luke 1:28 & 42)

6. **Read:** And had a wall great and high, and had twelve gates, and at the gates twelve angels, and names written thereon, which are the names of the twelve tribes of the children of Israel: (Revelation 21:12)

   Pray: Amen, come Lord Jesus! (Revelation 22:20)

   Say: Hail Mary, full of grace, the Lord is with thee. Blessed art thou among women, and blessed is the fruit of thy womb, Jesus. (Luke 1:28 & 42)

7. **Read:** And the wall of the city had twelve foundations, and in them the names of the twelve apostles of the Lamb. (Revelation 21:14)

   Pray: Amen, come Lord Jesus! (Revelation 22:20)

   Say: Hail Mary, full of grace, the Lord is with thee. Blessed art thou among women, and blessed is the fruit of thy womb, Jesus. (Luke 1:28 & 42)

8. **Read:** And I saw no temple therein: for the Lord God Almighty and the Lamb are the temple of it. (Revelation 21:22)

   Pray: Amen, come Lord Jesus! (Revelation 22:20)

Say: Hail Mary, full of grace, the Lord is with thee. Blessed art thou among women, and blessed is the fruit of thy womb, Jesus. (Luke 1:28 & 42)

9. **Read:** And the city had no need of the sun, neither of the moon, to shine in it: for the glory of God did lighten it, and the Lamb is the light thereof. (Revelation 21:23)
   Pray: Amen, come Lord Jesus! (Revelation 22:20)
   Say: Hail Mary, full of grace, the Lord is with thee. Blessed art thou among women, and blessed is the fruit of thy womb, Jesus. (Luke 1:28 & 42)

10. **Read:** And they shall bring the glory and honor of the nations into it. And there shall in no wise enter into it any thing that defileth, neither whatsoever worketh abomination, or maketh a lie: but they which are written in the Lamb's book of life. (Revelation 21:26-27)
   Pray: Amen, come Lord Jesus! (Revelation 22:20)
   Say: Hail Mary, full of grace, the Lord is with thee. Blessed art thou among women, and blessed is the fruit of thy womb, Jesus. (Luke 1:28 & 42)

Pray: Glory to God in the highest! (Luke 2:14)

Pray: Oh Jesus, meek and humble of heart, make our hearts like unto Thine. (Based on Matthew 11:29)

CLOSING PRAYER

We give Thee thanks, O Lord God Almighty,
Who is, and was, and is to come.
(Revelation 11:17)

Great and marvelous are Thy works, Lord God
Almighty;
just and true are Thy ways, Thou King of saints.
(Revelation 15:3)

Praise our God, all ye His servants,
and ye that fear Him, both small and great.
(Revelation 19:5)

Amen.
Even so, come, Lord Jesus.
The grace of our Lord Jesus Christ be with you all.
Amen.
(Revelation 22:20-21)

www.ingramcontent.com/pod-product-compliance
Lightning Source LLC
Chambersburg PA
CBHW071943020426
42331CB00010B/2993